ALCHEMY OF THE SOUL

ALCHEMY OF THE SOUL

Integral Healing:
The Work of Psychology and Spirituality

ARYA MALONEY

BLUE DOLPHIN PUBLISHING

Published by Blue Dolphin Publishing, Inc.
P.O. Box 8, Nevada City, CA 95959
Orders: 1-800-643-0765
Web: www.bluedolphinpublishing.com

Cover photo and author photo © 2004, James Erwin.

ISBN-13: 978-1-57733-172-8

Library of Congress Cataloging-in-Publication Data

Maloney, Arya, 1940–
    Alchemy of the soul : integral healing : the work of psychology and
spirituality / Arya Maloney.
        p. cm.
    Includes bibliographical references and index.
    ISBN-13: 978-1-57733-172-8 (pbk. : alk. paper)
    1. Consciousness. 2. Transpersonal psychology. 3. Psychology and
religion. 4. Ghose, Aurobindo, 1872-1950. I. Title.
    BF311.M25 2007
    150.19'8—dc22

                                                        2007003739

Printed in the United States of America

10   9   8   7   6   5   4   3   2   1

Dedication

To Sri Aurobindo and the Mother—
beloved teachers and psychologists of the highest order.

Table of Contents

Foreword

INTEGRAL PSYCHOLOGY is a phrase first coined by Indian psychologist Indra Sen in the 1930s and '40s to denote the psychology that emerged from Sri Aurobindo's integral yoga. Decades passed after Sen's pioneering work before other psychologists discovered the goldmine of psychological insights contained in Sri Aurobindo's integral yoga, and beginning in 2001 a series of international conferences have regularly convened to expand this work. Although still in embryonic form, integral psychology is now integrating the teachings of western psychology with the psychological knowledge of integral yoga. One key development of this movement is an integral approach to psychotherapy.

Although the term "integral" has achieved a certain popularity since then and come to include a wide variety of meanings, the present work comes out of the original lineage of integral psychology. Integral psychotherapy is both an integrating framework for the various schools of psychology, a kind of meta-psychology, as well as a theory and practice for working therapeutically. Each integral psychotherapist will, in keeping with the unique evolutionary line of each person, practice integral psychotherapy in a distinctive way.

In this book Arya Maloney has given us a beautifully crafted look into his work in integral psychotherapy. Beginning with a very personal and searingly honest sharing of his own journey, he then presents an overview of integral psychology's all-important context and theory—one that puts the soul (also called the psychic being) at the very center of integral psychology. Weaving together theory and clinical vignettes, he brings his work with clients alive in these pages. Freud once said that psychoanalysis could benefit more from a single case history well done than from volumes of theory. Arya Maloney proves this observation correct.

His sensitive, warm rendering of the subtleties and nuances of deep clinical work allow the reader a valuable glimpse into how the human psyche heals. His work with spiritual emergency and trauma will stand as a first in the growing literature of integral psychology, and a guidepost for those who follow. This is a wonderful book that significantly advances the field of integral psychology.

Brant Cortright, PhD
Director, Integral Counseling Psychology Program
California Institute of Integral Studies

Acknowledgments

GRATITUDE TO ARASI, beloved companion and friend of my soul, who has followed the entire process of this book using skillful means in the service of clarity and beauty of expression. Her unfailing support and encouragement were crucial to its completion.

Gratitude to Anandi, friend and editor par excellence. Merciless in slashing the purple prose of my writing, she, simultaneously, infused the work with her love and passion for its message. Anandi not only taught me to write, but also that writing is a powerful way to work on myself.

Gratitude to my children, Kathleen and Sean, for their loving support in my life.

Gratitude to Arnold Mindell, Aminah Raheem and Stan Grof for teaching me to mid-wife the great flow of consciousness pressing for manifestation in each being.

Gratitude to Paul Clemens of Blue Dolphin Publishing who believed in the work and the timeliness of its message.

Gratitude to my clients who have bestowed upon me myriad treasures from this adventure of consciousness.

Introduction:
The Encounter of Psychology
and Spirituality

EVOLUTION IN THE FIELD OF PSYCHOLOGY is radically altering the boundaries between psychology and spirituality. Psychology traditionally focuses on strengthening the ego. Spirituality, on the other hand, focuses on a reality beyond the ego in which states of higher consciousness emerge as the personality recedes. When personality withdraws, soul becomes apparent. As a therapist, I am witnessing this phenomenon. The once-separate domains of psychology and spirituality are interconnecting, creating a new paradigm of the human psyche.

The origin of this concept in Western psychology can be traced to the advent of *transpersonal* psychology in the late 1960s which linked traditional psychology's study of psyche with the less scientific exploration of soul. The repercussions of this pioneering is being experienced today by both clients and therapists as we stand on the threshold of an *evolving* psychology that has ventured beyond the borders of psychoanalysis, behaviorism and humanistic psychology into the domain of the sacred.

What truly defines the transpersonal orientation is a model of the human psyche that recognizes the importance of the spiri-

1

tual or cosmic dimensions and the potential for consciousness evolution. (Grof, 1985, p. 197)

A focus on higher states of consciousness stands in sharp contrast to the preoccupation of psychoanalysis and behaviorism with deficits in the human psyche. Though humanistic psychology has moved towards growth and self-actualization, many within this movement have begun to recognize its limits. Slowly, mystical experiences, transcendence, ecstasy and cosmic consciousness have entered the realm of psychology, opening the way to transpersonal psychology that acknowledges transcendental needs and spirituality as intrinsic aspects of human nature.

Transpersonal psychologists must build bridges between personality and spirit. Recognizing the devastation that can occur when soul manifests in an ego-centered world, skillful means must be used to guide travelers through their dark night—without short-circuiting this experience by hospitalization or drugs. Discriminating between psychotic and spiritual experience requires psychological and spiritual depth. Near-death journeys, past life memories, states of possession, unitive consciousness, shamanic states and awakening of the kundalini are transpersonal states which can be *mis*-diagnosed as psychotic episodes. Keenly aware of this danger, the transpersonal psychotherapist must guide the traveler through the narrow straits of personality into the wider realm of consciousness.

Ken Wilber, leading theoretician of transpersonal psychology, suggests that this new breed of guide, or "spiritual therapist," resembles the General Practitioner (GP) in Western medicine. This GP of the spirit

....should have at least a theoretical familiarity with all levels of the spectrum of consciousness—*matter, body, mind* (magic, mythic, rational, and integral-aperspectival); *soul* (psychic and subtle); and *spirit* (causal and non-dual). They should be familiar with the types of pathologies that can occur at each of these levels. They should be trained in the general lower techniques of bodily focusing and mental interpretation. They should know how to deal with persona, shadow and ego problems. And they should themselves have a specific higher or contemplative practice. (Wilber, 2000, p. 119)

Though not expected to personally practice all therapies, Wilber envisions the responsibilities of the transpersonal therapist as

- Practicing general psychotherapy and transpersonal therapy.
- Recommending specialists, if needed.
- Coordinating the client's tools of transformation.

Wilber's criteria for a spiritual therapist still remains largely unrealized because the training is demanding and lengthy. Therapists cannot learn solely through academic exploration or specialized training. They must probe the threads of their own personality and spirit: They must seek personal and *direct* knowledge of consciousness. To do this, regular, constant spiritual practice is imperative. Within the realms of transpersonal psychology, it is understood that spiritual states manifest not only in the zendo and the ashram, but also in the therapist's office. The therapist's breadth of vision, experience of transpersonal states, and discrimination can make the difference between a client entering a hospital or embracing his own spirituality.

Extensive mapping of states of consciousness, and the creation of inner technologies for accessing these states, have already been realized in the short life of transpersonal psychology. Pioneering therapists continue to expand this psychology by employing existing modalities and creating new ones. Instead of viewing human nature through the lens of pathology, the transpersonal therapist perceives it as a laboratory for the *evolution of consciousness* which emphasizes process rather than product. Transpersonal psychology exists as an open model rather than a closed system. Research into the evolution of consciousness continues to unfold as both client and therapist continue to uncover basic organic truths.

A New Paradigm of the Human Psyche

The Integral Yoga of Sri Aurobindo and the Mother is the ground on which I stand as a transpersonal therapist. While it is not within the scope of this book to fully investigate their vision, I will focus on their psycho-spiritual paradigm—a paradigm of evolutionary consciousness. This model of the human psyche can be more easily understood within the context of their personal history.

Sri Aurobindo was born on August 15, 1872, in Calcutta, India. His father, an anglicized Indian doctor prejudiced against Indian culture, sent his children to study in England. Hence, from the age of seven to twenty Sri Aurobindo studied at St. Paul's School and Cambridge University. During those thirteen years he received a thorough grounding in Western literature and civilization, receiving recognition as a brilliant scholar of Greek and Latin, as well as an accomplished poet. Returning to India in 1893, he taught at Baroda College, then became leader of an extremist political party striving to drive the British out of India. Through his revolutionary writing and oratory, he gained notoriety as "the most dangerous man in India." Arrested for conspiracy in May, 1908, he spent a year in prison. Though the British Government tried to convict him, he was acquitted and released in May 1909. His political activism continued, as did police harassment. His political career ended suddenly. Following what he called an *inner command*, he took refuge in the French Province of Pondicherry, arriving there on April 4, 1910. As his political life ended, his work of transformation of human nature began.

Sri Aurobindo achieved two major spiritual realizations during his public life—the experience of *nirvana* (the transcendent reality beyond name and form), and the experience of *cosmic consciousness* (the immanent Divine living in all forms). These experiences became the springboard for a new state of consciousness which, he claimed, sought liberation and unity not only in the hereafter, but *on the earth*—in the physical body. This state, which he called the *supramental,* was the next evolutionary stage—a stage in which all beings will possess a divine knowledge and power capable of transforming matter.

For the next forty years, Sri Aurobindo explored this work of transformation with his spiritual partner, the Mother.

Mother was born in Paris on February 21, 1878, and named Mirra Alfassa. She became aware of her deep and profound mission at the tender age of five. Later, between ages eleven and thirteen, psychic/spiritual experiences revealed her future: Many years before meeting Sri Aurobindo physically, she met him often in dreams, calling him "Krishna."

Gifted in mathematics, music and painting, Mirra befriended many of the great, contemporary Impressionist painters—Moreau, Rodin, Monet, before meeting Sri Aurobindo. She also studied the occult in Algeria with a Polish adept named Theon and his French wife, Alma. Study of supra-physical planes of consciousness led to her great spiritual ideal—*the bringing of Divine Consciousness into matter.* In 1914, Mirra visited Pondicherry with her husband, Paul Richard. Upon meeting Sri Aurobindo, she instantly recognized him as the "Krishna" of her dreams, and returned to Pondicherry on April 24, 1920 to begin their collaboration. After Sri Aurobindo's death in 1950, she continued their exploration of the "yoga of the cells"—a yoga leading to the total transformation of the body.

These spiritual explorers have given us a *new paradigm for a greater psychology*: This paradigm does not ignore the human physical or psychological nature, however, it goes beyond the egocentric focus of modern depth psychology as well as the etheric spiritualities which negate the possibility of transformation *on earth*. Even in the midst of his revolutionary thrust to free India from British rule, Sri Aurobindo turned to yoga for a greater knowledge and power, to *transform this world*.

> I am concerned with the earth, not with worlds beyond for their own sake; it is a terrestrial realization that I seek and not a flight to distant summits. (Sri Aurobindo, 2000, p. 124)

> The goal is not to lose oneself in the Divine Consciousness. The goal is to let the Divine Consciousness penetrate into Matter and transform it. (Mother, 1972-1987, 15:91)

This "terrestrial realization," this transformation of matter, gave rise to an *evolutionary spirituality*. Traditional yogas concentrated on unraveling the cords that bind soul and personality, ultimately releasing the disciple from life in this world. In the Integral Yoga of Sri Aurobindo and the Mother humanity is not the final rung in the evolutionary ladder; *it is a transitional species*. Just as the animal was the laboratory for the emergence of the human, so too *humankind* is the laboratory for the emergence of a *supramental species*. The supramental being reaches the heights of consciousness and then *descends* with this consciousness to the physical. As the Mother explains:

> When you are on the ascending path, the work is relatively easy. I had already covered that path at the beginning of the century and established a conscious relationship with the Supreme— with "That".... And "that" is what must be brought down into matter. This is the descending path, ... and there the work is immense. (Mother, 1951-1973, Vol. 1, p. 300)

The descending path of this new yoga is seemingly impossible, for here we confront human nature, universal nature, the body. The vast majority of spiritual seekers believe the body to be *unchangeable*, an obstacle to spiritual realization. In Sri Aurobindo's and Mother's yoga, however, the descending path brings Divine consciousness *into* the personality.

Adopting this perspective in psychotherapy opens possibilities for re-integration of states as diverse as the mystical and the traumatic. (See Chapter 3 in which we discuss practical applications.) *Individuality and individuation* do not disappear. Hence, spiritual realization does *not* discard psychology. It merely broadens its base. In uniting with the divine, neither individuality nor the process of individuation is lost. Beyond an *ego-centered individuality*, Sri Aurobindo and the Mother have given a new paradigm for a greater psychology, for a *soul-centered individuality—the next step in the science of psychology and in human evolution.*

To approach that layer of evolution that Sri Aurobindo calls "psychic transformation" is to approach the possibility of placing the soul at the center of the being and removing the ego, the personality from the center of the psychological universe. From this supposition questions arise. How does the soul affect the personality? How does the soul manifest in mind, body and emotions? As a transpersonal therapist, I have been fortunate to witness the soul's effect on personality. The case studies in this book are illustrations of this interface.

An Integral Approach to Healing

The Integral Yoga of Sri Aurobindo and the Mother, the basis of my work, is supported and complemented by the process-oriented psychology of Arnold Mindell; the holotropic breathwork of Stanislav and Christina Grof; and the process acupressure modality of Aminah Raheem. All of these modalities recognize transpersonal states of consciousness and utilize the body as a vehicle for accessing psycho-spiritual phenomena. Transpersonal practitioners Mindell, Grof and Raheem are deeply grounded in clinical psychology as well as Buddhism,

Taoism. Hinduism, Christianity, and their own spiritual practice. All are expert in discriminating between spiritual and psychotic experience. All are prototypes of the transpersonal guide. They offer an integral approach to healing that fully utilizes the body, life-force, mind and spirit. This integration aligns their psychology with the evolutionary psychology of Sri Aurobindo and the Mother.

Trained as a physicist and a Jungian analyst, Arnold Mindell studied the body's signals in both himself and in his clients. He discovered that a dream could be released to waking consciousness by amplifying an unconscious movement, sound or glance, or by exploring a physical symptom or feeling. The dream process then emerged as a phenomenon occurring in waking states, as well as sleeping ones. The body, Mindell discovered, dreams when awake.

He likened this discovery to the philosophy of Taoism. Like the work of following the Tao, following one's own psychological process results in a myriad of forms. It cannot, however, be defined by any of them: "The Tao that can be named is not the Great Tao." (Lao Tzu) By following our process, by following the Tao of our inner and outer world, we become more conscious of our personal history and of our transpersonal nature. Following one's process, unconsciously produced by the body, facilitates the process of individuation by leading beyond the dualistic world of *self* and *others*. This movement from ego to Self leads us to our true center. Mindell has created a transpersonal psychology which integrates mind, body and spirit.

Stanislav Grof, also a transpersonal pioneer, has focused on the use of breath to reveal psychological blocks and transpersonal states. His therapeutic modality, Holotropic Integration, is a further component of my work. Trained as a psychoanalyst in Czechoslovakia, Grof studied the then newly synthesized psychedelic, LSD—a drug simulating abnormal mind states. Questioning the slow, often unsuccessful process of psychoanalysis, he ingested the drug, hoping to induce these very states. His experience catapulted him into the arena of transpersonal psychology. Soon he received an offer to conduct research at a hospital in Baltimore, Maryland. After thousands of psychotherapeutic sessions (in which psychedelic substances were used), Grof found that his clients' experiences fell into one or more levels of consciousness: *Sensory*—expansion of sensory experience; *Perinatal*—experiences of birth and death; *Personal History*—experiences revealing childhood memories or trauma; *Transpersonal*—experiences of states of super-consciousness, i.e., ascent and descent of kundalini, past-life memories.

When the United States forbade researchers to use psychedelic substances, Grof and his wife, Christina, created *Holotropic Integration*. This technique, employing rapid breathing (hyperventilation), and loud, evocative music, produced altered states of consciousness similar to those induced by psychedelics. Like process-oriented psychology, holotropic breathwork is an integrative therapy involving body, mind, emotions and spirit. It is a modality which addresses the limits of personality, as well as the limitlessness of that which is beyond personality.

Aminah Raheem, an associate of Arnold Mindell and an innovator in the field of transpersonal psychology, combined classical acupressure with process-oriented psychology and created Transpersonal Integration. Though many practitioners of acupressure and acupuncture are aware of strong psychological, spiritual reactions in their clients, they have not been trained to work *consciously* with these reactions. Combining her experience with Mindell and her training in Jin Shin Jyutsu, she brought acupressure into the field of psychology. She began to follow the client's psycho-spiritual process while opening the energy of the body through acupressure.

Process acupressure works at the interface between personality and soul. It focuses either on personality or on soul issues. Recognizing that the body contains one's complete personal history, Raheem adds bodywork to transpersonal psychology, discovering that personal and soul psychology can be accessed through the body's energy points.

A Fourth Force

The soul-centered psychology offered in this book forges beyond the preoccupation of psychology with mind, emotions and body to a *fourth force*. With the advent of relativity and quantum theory, we no longer live in a three-dimensional world. The discovery of a space-time continuum has emerged. From the world of the new physics to the world of spiritual consciousness, reality is experienced as an interrelated whole—as the *fourth dimension*. Transpersonal psychology, which adds study of the soul to study of mind, emotions and body has become the *fourth force*, the next evolutionary step in the field of psychology.

This book is an offering to the ongoing research of transpersonal psychology and to those individuals curious about a soul-centered psychology which opens the way to a higher consciousness. In my experience, the evolutionary paradigm of Sri Aurobindo and the Mother, coupled with the transpersonal approaches of Mindell, Grof and Raheem, forge a psychotherapeutic approach capable of integrating body, life-force, mind, soul and spirit.

Part 1 introduces a soul-centered psychology that creates bridges between psychotherapy and spiritual practice. Part II contains the stories of four of my clients, illustrating the power of *integral psychotherapy* to address multiple life situations.

PART I

INTEGRAL PSYCHOLOGY

1

Spontaneity of Soul:
An Autobiographical Glimpse

AT AGE FIVE I received my first formal teaching on the relationship between body and soul. In a catechism class taught by Roman Catholic nuns, I was informed that my reason for existence was to save my immortal soul. If I succeeded in controlling my body's desires on earth, my soul would achieve eternal bliss in heaven. If I did not succeed, I would endure eternal separation from God. I was assured, nevertheless, that my body would be mysteriously resurrected and would eventually rejoin my soul at the end of the world.

Despite this promise of resurrection, I was left with the terrifying impression that body and soul were separate. I was to *believe* in the soul and work for its salvation—but not to *experience* it until after I died. Unable to sense a vital meaning in this convoluted message, my young mind grappled rebelliously with this injunction.

Fortunately, I had already felt the presence of my soul and continued to experience it with amazing regularity in spite of this formidable imprint.

Though the church left its mark, the mark left by my parents was deeper. My father had been coerced into marrying my eighteen-year-old, pregnant mother. Both were severely alcoholic and neither was capable of caring for a child. After three stormy years, my father left.

During the first three years of my life, I experienced fear, hunger and physical discomfort. My parents' physical and psychological absence exacerbated my instinct for survival. With no human presence to comfort me, I turned, in my need, to a deep unseen presence. Calling to my mother's sodden, unconscious form as I stumbled through a dark, empty apartment, I sensed a greater self guiding me.

I sensed the presence of my soul.

When I was three, just before my father left, I walked away from our apartment complex in Buffalo, New York. My parents later referred to this episode as my being "lost." I was not lost. Young as I was, I left *intending* to escape the unbearable pain of my life. As my small legs carried me away, I experienced an enormous sense of freedom. Though eventually two policemen returned me to my parents, I remember that as I rode in the squad car I was overcome with an inexplicable sense of new-found freedom.

Shortly after, my father abandoned my mother and myself by joining the army. We moved to my grandmother's house. As I entered the sane space of my grandmother's world, I was at last able to escape the chaos of living with two alcoholics. My mother continued to drink, but never in her mother's home. Each afternoon she disappeared with her current drinking partner, not returning until the early morning hours. She would sleep, then begin again the drunken cycle. Though I suffered periods of turmoil, for the most part I lived under the fierce protective love and care of my grandmother.

The joy I experienced during this period stands out in sharp contrast to the misery triggered by my mother's abandonment. This ecstatic state emerged dramatically one day as I explored my grandmother's land.

Abandonment made me adept at playing alone. I would trek eagerly from my grandmother's kitchen through the dark woodshed and down the dirt path that led round the back of the house, continuing across the lawn and up the incline that led to a small outbuilding called the "honey-house."

My body was alive with sensation. I was aware of the comforting kitchen odors, the woodshed's fragrance, the fresh air's caress. I felt the weight of the massive wooden door, the solidity of the hard-packed dirt floor, the change of terrain as I left the lawn and entered the pasture's taller grass. Simultaneously, I became aware of a burgeoning exhilaration, anticipation and joy. Upon entering the old, crumbling honey-house, I was enveloped by its sweet, sharp fragrance. Entranced, I observed the dance of a million minuscule particles magnified by the sun's filtered rays. For the first time in my young life I was plunged into a world of oneness. My usual feelings of separation, fear and sadness vanished. An ecstatic energy erased all boundaries, revealing honey, ancient wood, sun and dust as members of my own body.

Beyond the honey-house, a vast boulder-strewn pasture beckoned. Ascending one of the giants, I nestled in a lichen-filled hollow and surveyed my kingdom. Here the dew, the eternal drone of the honey-gatherers, the wildflower perfume, all conspired to banish time and space from my consciousness.

Descending, I soon came upon my favorite companion—the rushing brook. Mesmerized by the sight of minnows, dragon flies and colored rocks, I stripped off my clothing and leaped in. Instantly, my overheated body became one with the cool water. Only the sound of my grandmother's voice calling me to lunch was able to return me to ordinary reality.

Although I attended church, this world of honey and boulders and stream became the true temple of my soul. Here joy and ecstasy inhabited my bodily senses. I was no longer separate: I was an integral part of *one* enlarged body. This altered sense of reality, which, perhaps, all children experience, this earliest consciousness of the soul, has manifested itself many times in my lifetime. It invades my ordinary consciousness *spontaneously*. It reveals itself independently of my own will. Contrary to the church's teaching, it enhances my awareness of "body" in *this* lifetime.

This body-soul intimacy is not to be confused with reverie, trance or meditation. In these latter states, consciousness momentarily leaves the physical body. *Transcending* the body, it separates from the field of physical awareness, often leaving the body without sensation.

In my early childhood adventures, my soul-infused body not only amplified all my sensations, but transcended my ordinary perception of its limits. I *did not leave* my physical body: I inhabited it *in a new way*, becoming one with "other bodies," like the stream or the high grass. Years later, however, my consciousness began to identify with my developing mind, and my soul became temporarily veiled.

I was wrenched from my grandmother's protective love at age six. My mother's liaison with another man took us into an era which I think of as "the ten-year-war." Seated in the back of my stepfather's car, I waved for the last time to my beloved granny. Not wanting to cry, I stared straight ahead. The man and woman sitting in front of me appeared strange and ominous. My stepfather's shaven head and porcine features chilled me. My mother's disheveled hair and blank gaze sent my stomach plummeting. Intuitively, I perceived the shadows of the dark world I was about to enter.

From age six to sixteen I served a sentence in my stepfather's "prison." This "prison" was a large dairy farm on which I was forced to work daily from four in the morning until eight in the evening. Vacations or overnights with friends were nonexistent; my only respite was the time spent in school. My stepfather eradicated any tendency towards laziness with his brutality. My mother, an inmate in her own right, passively witnessed the abuse I suffered.

This ten-year battle with my sadistic tormenter trained me in the art of contacting my soul. Recognizing his desire to break me, mentally, emotionally and physically, I was forced to turn in-ward. This strategy had to be skillfully employed since any withdrawal remotely resembling defiance would invite more abuse.

I learned how to please my captor through my capacity for physical work. Ignoring my academic performance, he re-sponded only to my ability to match him (and his hired hands) in the arduous process of operating a large farm. Three hours before school, three hours after school, twelve-hour days of hard labor on weekends and vacations, became the rhythm of my life. Any deviation from this immutable schedule invited both physical and psychological abuse. My ordinary ways of being in the world— the clothing I wore, the food I ate, the praise I received from others—only opened me further to the sadistic denigration of this demon.

While my passage through this bizarre world of slavery, drunken brawls and brutality was eased by a strong mind and body, it was my grandmother's love and that wider, indestruc-tible "Self" discovered in her pasture, that saved me. Drawing strength from this core, I looked into the eyes of my enemy and knew he could not break me.

One day, at age twelve, after suffering severe humiliation at the hands of my stepfather, I paced the driveway in silent rage: In this dark moment I heard a clear, inner command, "You must leave this place or you will die." Within months of this command my natural father reappeared after an absence of nine years. He stayed only a few minutes, but those minutes opened the way to a short vacation with him—a vacation which further kindled my inner rebellion.

At age sixteen, during a rare respite from work, I was for the first time allowed to visit my maternal grandfather. Tasting this brief liberation, I asked to live with him. He agreed. I wrote to my mother who, true to her passivity and indifference, did not question my decision. At age sixteen, I at last escaped from a decade of slavery.

Though living with an alcoholic grandfather was far from idyllic, I experienced once again the freedom of a self-directed life. Simply not to be dragged from my bed at four in the morning seemed a miracle! The absence of constant abusive commentary allowed my nervous system to relax. Living without a "gun at my head" filled me with a quiet joy.

My last two years of high school were pervaded by this sense of liberation. College became a possibility, a means to transcend the limitations of my family. Shamed by the economic and cultural poverty of my past, motivated by promise of employment, I was drawn to the study of science. I chose chemistry as a vehicle to lead me to freedom.

I worked in a glass factory thirty hours a week, double shifts during summers, while I earned a Bachelor of Science degree. (My apprenticeship in my stepfather's workhouse had served me well!) Marriage and entrance into a Ph.D. program in physical organic chemistry followed undergraduate school. Yet, even as I pursued course work, comprehensive exams and experimental research, I became aware of an overwhelming interest in religion and philosophy. After much consideration, I left the path of science to study philosophy and religion.

For the next ten years, I was immersed in the academic world. Teaching courses as diverse as organic chemistry, Christian theology and Indian philosophy helped me to support a wife and two small children, as well as graduate studies. At the same time, I joined my students in a search for truth, and joined the anti-war movement. Throughout my graduate studies I maintained my identity with the Roman Catholic church. Simultaneously, however, with the growth of political consciousness and awareness of grave contradictions in the church's teaching, this identity dissolved. The church could no longer nourish me spiritually.

During my twenty-ninth year my father contracted cancer. He was in my care for the last six months of his life. This passage led to a deep healing of our relationship. It also radically transformed my life. As I witnessed the diminishment of his body, I became keenly aware, not only of his death, but *of my own*: I knew, viscerally, that I, too, was dying. My life, seemingly so substantial until now, had grown empty.

On the day of my father's burial, I stepped onto a college picket line in protest of the Vietnam War. This strike led to the temporary closing of the college where I taught, thus radically transforming my life. Driven to discover a deeper reality, I now plunged into acts of civil disobedience against racism and poverty; and, above all, against our involvement in Vietnam. Experimentation with psychedelic drugs, meditation and trance induction followed. Not only was my external world altered, my psyche was also. Previously unexplored—I became aware of realms subconscious and superconscious.

These potent experiences, between 1968 and 1972, completely altered the direction of my life. My youthful marriage was crumbling, as was my relationship with academia. The college's failure to renew the contract of a politically controversial colleague in 1970 prompted my resignation. I secured a position in the philosophy department of another university and discovered Eastern spirituality. A statement by Carl Jung (the great Swiss psychiatrist) connecting self-discovery and yoga, triggered my spiritual search. It led me to the Integral Yoga of Sri Aurobindo, the renowned Indian yogi who taught the spiritual transformation of the physical body, and the Mother, his spiritual partner.

Fascinated by the correlation between drug-induced states of consciousness and classical mystical experience, I decided to write my doctoral dissertation on this correlation. During this period, 1970 to 1972, I also became aware of Jean Houston's and Robert Master's work on altered states of consciousness. After reading their *Varieties of Psychedelic Experience* and *Mind Games,* I volunteered to be a research subject. In this experiment, trance-like effects were induced through movement and guided imagery. As a result, I experienced what felt like a powerful initiation from an inner figure—an old man with long white hair and beard, wearing an Indian *dhoti* (a cloth that wraps around the waist and drapes over one shoulder). In his presence, I experienced a rush of energy travelling from the base of my spine up and out the top of my head.

I identified this figure as the "Wise Old Man," a Jungian archetype symbolizing the true Self. Another year was to pass before I recognized the "Wise Old Man" as Sri Aurobindo.

Soon after, however, I could no longer enter these inner worlds. Then, on my thirty-second birthday, a friend gave me a compilation of Sri Aurobindo's writings. Compelled by the power of his vision, I immediately purchased eight volumes of his work. I realized that Sri Aurobindo was the mystic in my vision and the focus of my dissertation.

Recognizing that my "failure" to go into trance signaled a need to alter my course, Jean Houston, at that time my mentor, said, "If you are going to write about Sri Aurobindo, why not go to his ashram in India?" As she spoke, I knew I must go. In a matter of months, I was on my way.

Thus began the journey that radically transformed my life.

Granted a six-month sabbatical from the university, I applied for an Indian visa. I was told that I had to receive my visa from an Indian Consulate in Europe, then continue to India. My daily phone calls met with disappointment—no visa. I rented a small room in Amsterdam and spent days in the local library reading Sri Aurobindo's vast works. Steeping myself in his consciousness, I came to know *experientially* what the great sage calls *cit-sakti*, consciousness-force, the power of the Mother (the feminine aspect of God). *Cit-sakti* awakened an energy that propelled me nightly through the streets of Amsterdam: I walked for miles along the canals; but not in my ordinary consciousness. It was as if an autonomous energy was "walking me." Replaced by a conscious, inexhaustible force, "I" became insubstantial, on the verge of disappearing.

During the day, however, "I" returned with a vengeance. "What if the visa is not granted? My money is running out! Time is running out! I don't have any control over this matter!" Identification with this "I" triggered a state of instant anxiety—the polar opposite of my evening state. One morning, I miraculously received an inner visitation from the Mother. "Do not worry, I will take care of everything." Though I looked forward eagerly to meeting the Mother in the Pondicherry ashram (spiritual center), I was terrified. Sri Aurobindo's yoga of surrender to the Mother had triggered the shadow-experiences of my own alcoholic mother as well as my images of a passive and weak Virgin Mary.

A profound calm descended. A sudden energy arose in my body as well as the knowledge that with or without a visa I must travel to India immediately. Despite India's immigration practice of barring those without visas, I somehow knew the Mother would take care of *everything*. At New Delhi airport, I was fiercely interrogated. "You are breaking the law! We must put you on the next return flight!" Quietly, I told my story. Mysteriously, the chief officer softened and granted me a ten-day transit visa. As soon as I arrived, I felt completely at home in India. An official in the State Department became very interested in my quest and, after a long conversation about spiritual realization, promised to *personally* look into the matter of my visa. After ten days in Nepal, I was granted a visa to return to India.

Journeying via New Delhi, I arrived in Pondicherry on the anniversary of Sri Aurobindo's birthday. I experienced Mother's physical presence or *darshan* (transmission of divine consciousness) at the ashram, but by this time I had experienced many *inner* darshans which revealed the power of soul and the transparency of the human personality.

Slowly, she was opening the way.

I remained in the ashram from August 15 until December 21, 1973. On November 17, Mother left her physical body. Weeks later I attended a slide show of Mother's life. A photograph of her descending a staircase, startlingly, came to life for me. With this, a pillar of intense energy entered the crown of my head: Descending through my spine and legs into the earth, anchoring my consciousness in my body, it also catapulted me far beyond it.

Enveloped by this force field, I continued to watch the slide show. The last image faded from the screen. The lights came on. I rose with my companion, left the theatre and set off through the streets of Pondicherry. Moving through the cool, jasmine-scented air, I became aware of a strange effortlessness. This harmony of motion manifested in the frictionless rotation of my shoulder joints, the synchronization of my arms and legs, the undulation of my spine and the sway of my pelvic girdle as it balanced my shifting weight. I experienced myself as a well-oiled machine powered by an inexhaustible source of energy. Possessed by this ecstasy, I was completely unaware of the speed at which I was traveling until my companion cried out, "Why are we in such a rush?" Awakened to my swift, harmonious strides, I reveled in this joy of movement. Simultaneously, with this awareness came the astral experience of being in many locations at the same time—South India, the United States, Afghanistan.

For the next three days I continued to be moved by this pillar of energy. I was pervaded by a joy I had never known before. Previously, I had experienced the *ascent* of kundalini energy—from the base of my spine to the crown of my head. This *descent* of energy, a reverse kundalini, which had been triggered by the image of the Mother descending the staircase produced currents of energy that streamed through my arms, legs, torso and head.[1] These currents reduced my body's density and created a lightness and plasticity. Persistent pressure in the area of my heart unleashed emotions of joy, ecstasy, longing and gratitude. My tears flowed with abandonment. I became sensitized to the emotional states of others. Even as I felt them in my own body, I realized that they were part of a larger energy field. As if by divine fiat, my

---

1. Kundalini energy is the conscious energy responsible for the manifestation of all form in the universe; human beings are microcosms of the universe in which the potential energy (kundalini) that is not being used for the maintenance of the being is stored in the base of the spine; all spiritual evolution involves an actualization of this energy.

narrow self-absorbed identity had been replaced by a soul identity. The veil of separation had been temporarily lifted.

During the following days I read Sri Aurobindo's epic poem, SAVITRI and was drawn to the canto, "The Way of Fate and the Problem of Pain." This canto describes the role of pain—in the evolution of consciousness, and in the realization of the soul. As I read, each line triggered new sensations. His words became windows into a sea of consciousness, and I could feel their truth in the cells of my body.

Gradually, the intensity of this consciousness diminished. Its imprint, however, remained, paralleling the childhood imprint received at age three. These experiences and others have become beacons, guiding me steadily towards a reconciliation of personality and soul, permanently altering my vision of healing. For me, they have eradicated all doubt about the union of body and soul, affirming the manifestation of soul *in* the physical body. Returning to the West at the end of 1973, my focus as a psychotherapist radically shifted. Integrating the body, I no longer work exclusively with the mind and emotions.

In 1977, once again in India, I experienced further soul intervention. My partner during this period had become attracted to another man. Filled with a wild mixture of anger, sadness, anxiety and depression, I cycled to the Samadhi (a courtyard where Sri Aurobindo and the Mother are buried and people gather to meditate and offer flowers). Unable to sit, I was reduced to a frantic pacing. Breathing became rapid and shallow, my chest tight. A gnawing emptiness penetrated stomach and intestines. Envious of those seated in meditation, the best I could manage were brief moments of staring into space. Suddenly, pushing from within, an intense pressure invaded my heart. Immediately, the intense anxiety and depression lifted, and energy currents streamed through my body. Fear and contraction vanished. Suffused with gratitude for the pure act of existence, waves of love swept through me. I experienced the universal heart, realizing both animate and inanimate entities are *part of a larger body*. As if by divine fiat, my narrow, self-absorbed identity had been replaced by a soul-identity. The veil of separation had been temporarily lifted, revealing a cosmic web of energy.

Mounting my bicycle, I left the Samadhi and set off through the streets of Pondicherry. The intensity of the sun, as well as my own inner state, was tempered by a cool sea breeze. Where was the wretch who, barely an hour before, had been agitated beyond belief?

Altered states of consciousness diminish. The walls of the ego return as do anger, sadness and anxiety, however, the remembrance of the soul's freedom remains.

The gifts received, whether in my grandmother's pasture or in India, have made me understand that I do not have to *leave* my physical body in order to experience my soul. Body, mind and emotions are instruments of the soul. The manifestation of the soul in the body unveils the role of each in the larger energy field.

If the soul is the integrator and healer, then spiritual practice is the means of opening the mind, body and emotions to its power. Much of spiritual practice, both Eastern and Western, aspires to either *use* body, mind and emotions in order to reach the soul, or abandon all three in order to reach this goal. The Integral Yoga of Sri Aurobindo and the Mother, however, acts *on* the body, mind and emotions—empowering *them*, making *them* conscious instruments of the soul.

My experiences have radically altered my vision of psychotherapy. I have realized that the soul can break through *in emotionally taxing times* as well as calm periods. The serious quest for the limitless soul requires a serious investigation of the limited personality. This exploration requires awareness, and quite often healing. It is the role of the soul in this healing process that draws me to further investigations.

Dwelling for years in a house, we suddenly discover a great central, connecting room. Discovery of this central room in the house of psychology will create a major revolution in our understanding of healing.

CHAPTER

2

The Body and
Psycho-Spiritual Process

In Buddhism we call the body/mind formation *namarupa*.
Namarupa is the psyche-soma, the mind-body as one entity... If
we can overcome the duality that sees the mind and body as
entirely separate, we come very close to the truth. (Thich Nhat
Hanh, 2001, p. 14)

Body work extends the experiential dimension of dreams and
generally increases the possibility for knowing the unconscious.
On the other hand, dream work gives body processes a per-
sonalized, visual structure which—as far as I know—they have
never had before in therapeutic work. (Mindell, 1982, p. 199)

When the material mentality is seized with an idea, it is actually
possessed by the idea and it's almost impossible for it to free
itself. Diseases are just that. It's the same thing with Parkinson's
disease: this tremor is the possession by an idea, it's what in the
conscious intelligence is expressed as the possession by an idea,
a hypnosis accompanied by a fear in matter.... And The Body's
Cells Obey That Material Mind. (Mother, cited in Satprem,
1982, pp. 86-7)

THOUGH MOST MAINSTREAM PSYCHOLOGY does not focus on the
body, the body and mind are not separate entities. The patterns

25

of matter and the patterns of mind are interwoven, so that mental vibrations create cellular changes and cellular changes create mental vibrations. *Mind, body, spirit* can be differentiated in this vast energy field only by their particular vibrational frequencies.

This assertion is accepted among modern physicists as well as by those doing psychological and spiritual work. Albert Einstein perceived this energetic unity:

> We may regard matter as being constituted by the regions of space in which the field is extremely intense.... There is no place in this new kind of physics, both for the field and matter, for the field is the only reality. (Einstein, 1991, p. 211)

This paradigm shift—from perceiving and experiencing the world as an assemblage of solid objects separated by empty space, to perceiving it instead as a vast energy field containing transitory forms of varying vibrations—necessitates a re-evaluation of *all* fields of endeavor. An *integral psychology*, sees body, life force, mind, soul and spirit as interdependent, co-existing as energetic structures differentiated only by vibrational frequencies. The work of integrating the body-mind in therapeutic practice was marked by the formation in 1966 of the U.S. Association for Body Psychotherapy—an organization of psychotherapists and body-workers who focus on the body through dance and massage therapy, psychodrama, bioenergetics, Rubenfeld Synergy. With this collective effort a movement is at last underway to integrate bodywork with psychotherapy. In addition many acupuncturists, physical therapists and somatic practitioners have begun to attend to the psychological process in their work.

With present widespread interest in such books as Thomas Moore's *Care of the Soul* and James Hillman's *The Soul's Code* we are witnessing a contemporary movement to integrate mind-body-emotions into the healing process. Following this momentum would inevitably lead to the *master integrator, the soul*. As the scientific and psychological recognition of *oneness* emerges, our approach to the healing of mind, body, spirit and world must change radically. Our survival and our ongoing evolution are at stake.

A new psychology which recognizes the centrality of soul in the healing process will discover that contact with this center
- can be directly accessed through the body.
- amplifies the healing of mental, emotional and physical problems.
- extends the capacities of mind, emotions and body.
- integrates mind, body and emotions.
- liberates us from identification with mind, body and emotions.
- bridges psychotherapy and spiritual practice.
- reveals an interdependent universe.

This soul centrality *manifests* through mental, emotional and physical vehicles. But the mind, limited in its power, cannot lead in the creation of this new psychology. Along with the emotions and the body, the mind must make way for the soul to emerge as master of our being. Inviting soul into the therapeutic process is comparable to standing at the edge of a virgin forest. Since the terrain is unknown, we must proceed slowly as we open to the influx of soul, to its power to expand and transform.

The Dreaming Body

While teaching a course on the role of the body in psychotherapy, I asked the students to write about a recurring childhood dream and/or memory. Based on Arnold Mindell's discovery of the intimate connection between chronic physical symptoms and early dreams, this exercise was inspired by the teachings of Carl Jung. Childhood dreams, he claimed, are like personal myths; they serve as blueprints for long-term life patterns. Extending his mentor's claim, Mindell observed that early childhood dreams not only manifest in adulthood, but actually create symptoms in the body: Chronic symptoms can actually be found lurking in recurring childhood dreams! These symptoms, eventually manifesting in our bodies, boldly infer that mind and matter are reflections of one another.

Exploring these concepts with the group, I asked if someone would share an early childhood dream or memory. Liz raised her hand. She recalled an early dream which she had many times as a child. She remembered waking in terror, inconsolable and trembling. In this dream, she and her mother dressed elegantly for an excursion to the Castle Theater. Once there, she played in the ornate ladies dressing room while her mother went into a stall. Suddenly, gangsters with machine guns stormed the bathroom and shot through the closed lavatory door. After the assault, the little girl saw her mother's blood flow downward into the drain.

As Liz related this dream she trembled and fought back tears. Yet even as the dream re-ignited her terror, her personality discounted her emotions. Her words fitful, body shaking uncontrollably, she related the early childhood memory:

> My parents had a terrible argument. After, my father shoved my mother, and broke a wall with his fist, he sped out of the driveway in our brown Chevy. My mother and I were deeply shaken. Would he return before we could escape?
>
> I remember that we dressed in fine clothes. Our appearance, however, did not alleviate our distress. It was a desolate, cold Sunday. We were nearly at the bus stop when a car approached. I tugged at my mother, Mommy! Hurry up, run!" Then I heard his voice, "Get in the car."
>
> Shaking and crying, I hid under my mother's soft skirts. I fell asleep instantly and remembered having a happy dream. But when I awoke and saw him in the front seat, I remembered with despair my life with them. My mother said it was all right; he wouldn't hurt us. It wasn't true!

In relating her story, however, she continued to cling to her survival self. She verbally minimized her terror:

I felt as though I was standing on top of a tall building, and the others in the class were on ground level. My shaking invaded my entire body. I was a mess. However, I tried to hide by saying I don't need help. I help others, and I should shut the fuck up!

Liz's mother had impeccably trained her daughter not only to care for their abuser, *but to ignore the abuse*. However, as Liz's body memory betrayed her, her violent trembling became autonomous.

It felt as though I was being pulled inward; that my soul was seeking to hide itself in the far reaches of my body. Like a rubbery substance, it bounded back and forth, forcing me to shake.

Liz spent the remaining class time in the terrifying world of her childhood. Both the dream and the early memory had revealed the co-existence of two radically different worlds. In the dream the ornate, ostentatious Castle Theater is the setting of murder. In the memory, she and her mother dally, decorating themselves when they must run for their lives.

To verify Mindell's discovery, we focused on the connection between Liz's recurring childhood dream and her chronic physical symptoms of Raynaud's Syndrome:

My fingers go numb and cannot move. The dream and memory have made themselves known in my fingers. The blood drains from my hands—the way I pull my spirit back into the recesses of my body. When I feel fear, I go numb.

Liz's dream of her mother's death is the visual blueprint of a life-long psychological pattern of abuse and helplessness. This pattern manifests in her body. Blood draining from her hands—Raynaud's Syndrome—is visualized in the dream as blood flowing into the bathroom drain. As her life-force pulls inward, Liz's fingers turn blue. She realized that she re-experiences this moment whenever she confronts an authority figure.

Liz was surprised at the resurgence of these memories and the powerful reactions they produced in her body. However, it seemed as though pieces of a puzzle were coming together, therefore she meditated on this past event and the feelings that had been submerged but *not* eradicated. In meditation she recreated her childhood memory—the violent fight, the attempted escape, and the forced return to the back seat where she fell asleep: "After falling asleep with my head tucked beneath my mother's soft skirt, I remembered being lifted by gentle, invisible 'hands'. Instantly, I felt safe." In re-living this trauma a gift was revealed. Liz re-experienced the transpersonal dimension she had forgotten. Both the trauma and its transpersonal counterpart continued to live in the cells of her body.

Beginning with mental exploration of her early childhood dream and memory, Liz processed all parts of her being—physical, emotional, mental and transpersonal. When amplification of a life threatening childhood memory led to a corresponding bodily reaction—shaking and trembling—Liz experienced Thich Nhat Hanh's teaching: "*Namarupa* is the psyche-soma, the mind-body as one entity..." (Thich Nhat Hanh, 2001, p. 14)

This trauma also opened her to the transpersonal realm, and she remembered being lifted into a protected world where joy replaced fear. Accessing trauma often leads to realms of spirit. Working with numerous victims of trauma, I have repeatedly witnessed this 'miracle'—the body in trauma is not only a container for terror, but a catalyst for joy.

Liz's journey traversing the full spectrum of her being, constitutes an *integral approach to healing*.

Kundalini Energy and Aversion

In a therapeutic setting, contacting the body can *rapidly* elicit strong emotions—energy flows strong enough to create involuntary movements. Maria suffered from a lifetime of depression. A creative person, she was unable to work. Though loving her husband, she avoided sexual contact. She suffered from muscle pain, severe digestive problems and low energy. During a series of extended process acupressure sessions, however, Maria experienced huge uprisings of energy in the lower part of her spine (first and second chakras), and was startlingly transformed from her depressed, low energy state to a state of terror. With each jolt, she jumped and shook uncontrollably. Hyperventilation, punctuated by periods of screaming and crying, conveyed the impression of torture. Eventually, these explosions propelled her from a horizontal position into perpetual movement about the room. Wringing her hands, she alternated between pacing from window to window, to assuming a fetal position. She was inconsolable.

Becoming quiet, Maria closed her eyes. Visualizing herself in another time and space, she realized that a past life memory was emerging:

> I am a young, beautiful woman living in an Eastern, or Asian, country. Lavishly dressed, I am a concubine whose only purpose is to please my master sexually. My shoes have turned-up toes and are embroidered with butterflies and flowers. Servants dress me; I am served the best food, massaged and instructed in erotic techniques. Since I am blindfolded, I do not see who is having sex with me; but I am aware that his pleasure extends far beyond mine. I am stimulated until pleasure becomes torture.
>
> I remember my room, its large bed embroidered with beautiful white and gold silk fabric. The floors are perfectly smooth. There is a table and a window. Sounds of people reach my ears, but I am not allowed to look out; nor am I allowed to speak to anyone, or do anything other than look beautiful and be prepared for sex with the master. Suicide is my only escape.

Coming out of trance, Maria felt great shame. Unable to look at me, she repeatedly whispered, "I'm sorry. I hate myself." The intensity of this experience impelled Maria to explore further.

She contacted a noted psychic who helped in police investigations. Her notes on that meeting shed light on her unexplained reaction:

> He told me that I had a past life as a concubine in China and that I had been bought at a very young age by a rich master. Though he loved me, he expected me to be a sexual slave. I hated this life and his control so much I committed suicide.

At last Maria realized that she had been defending herself against attack her entire life. She veiled her body as well as her creative force and avoided contact with others. Suffering from severe fibromyalgia and chronic fatigue, she was unable to work. During this time, however, her dreams aided her healing process:

> I am living in a city. Everything, including my factory-like apartment, is dilapidated and gray. While attending a spiritual group my qualifications are questioned, but a young man is kind to me.
>
> Home again, I take a shower. Then I go into the drab kitchen to get some food from a half-size refrigerator. The whole environment is colorless and dark.
>
> The young man comes to visit. He is very loving; he understands me. He wants to help me get accepted by the spiritual group. I am attracted to him. He leaves and I lift my special, long dress, checking a tumor the size of a grapefruit on the inside of my left knee. I had grown so accustomed to it, I had forgotten it was there! It is a bulbous growth, six inches in diameter, with an opening on the top. Peering inside, I see muscle and mucous, its center filled with white pus. Touching it, the mucous sticks to my fingers, forming long gooey strings. I become immobile.

The dream's dark, sterile environment reflects Maria's undernourished life and her isolation—even from the man she loves. A talented artist, she has blocked her creative force. The

kind young man in the dream represents her masculine energy
(animus)—the energy that makes contact with the world and
manifests one's vision of life. He offers this energy to help her out
of hiding and to pursue her spiritual path, Tibetan Buddhism.
Both her aspiration, and her obstacle to achieving it, are reflected
in her dream.

Maria's fear of men and the world is exacerbated by her past-
life experience as a concubine. Although attracted to the young
man in the dream, she conceals herself. How could she make love
with him? He will see her condition.

The tumor, an obstacle to her feminine and sexual energy,
resembles a phallus, and reflects her disgust for sex. Despite its
size, and its effect on her mobility, she has grown "accustomed"
to it. Mirroring her habitual repression of the subconscious, her
"special, long dress" hides her condition from herself and the
world.

I encouraged Maria to draw the tumor and be aware of the
emerging images and feelings:

As I draw, I am both sick and nervous. The tumor is like a flower
bud trying to explode, or bloom; but it is infected with bugs.
Sometimes it feels like an explosion of sexual energy. It makes
me weak. It sucks all energy and creativity out of me.

In an imaginal dialogue with the tumor, she wrote:

Maria: What if I shrink you, slowly? What if I kill you!
Tumor: I can't let you kill me. I enjoy my purpose—to create
pain in your legs and feet; to suck your life energy, and impede
your movements.
Maria: Get off me! I feel your weight, but I'm not strong enough
to push you off. You depress me and I want to kill myself. I feel
a tremendous energy emerging between my navel and spine. I
want to move, but I'm afraid. I feel like Siamese twins: One has
to die for the other to live.

Caught between too much energy and none, Maria battles for a creative, meaningful life. Attempts to dance, sculpt and make love have triggered fear and panic. Years of isolation, physical pain, exhaustion and depression have pushed her dangerously close to the precipice of despair while a burgeoning energy which she tries to hide (like the tumor's out-of-control cells in her dream) threatens her precarious control. Remarkably, she has regained enough strength to go to school and work part time but must battle daily with patterns that block her full engagement with and enjoyment of life.

In Maria's case, her psychological process opened up in a therapeutic session. This unwanted energy caused her to experience strong, involuntary movements, hyperventilation, and the transpersonal awareness of a past life. Activated in our therapy session, kundalini energy, housed in the base of the spine, propelled her movements and reactivated memories of a past life of sexual abuse.

Kundalini Energy and Ecstasy

As in Maria's case, activation of the kundalini can initiate a *psycho-spiritual process in the body.* Depending on identification with or aversion to one's experience, the flow of kundalini can evoke either agony or ecstasy. With Maria, it was capable of thrusting psychological complexes into consciousness. Once awakened, this energy acts autonomously.

Kundalini can also produce an ecstatic expansion of consciousness beyond the ordinary boundaries of human experience. While meditating in the presence of Swami Muktananda, an Indian kundalini master, I experienced its astonishing power.

During a meditation, he circulated among the participants, transmitting *shaktipat (kundalini energy)* through touch, glance and thought. When he stood close to me, I instantly and involuntarily began to hyperventilate: Energy coursed up my spine, down my arms and legs and up into my head. Accompanied by explosions of light, heat and pressure increased throughout my body. I had been connected to a high voltage generating station. For what seemed an eternity, the kundalini held sway over me. She coursed through my body, mind and emotions—obliterating boundaries, bequeathing oneness. Gradually, my breathing returned to normal. When I opened my eyes, colors seemed brighter; forms emerged with new clarity; heightened energy coursed through my entire body.

In my therapeutic practice, I have witnessed kundalini's activation in various clients. One of the manifestations of kundalini energy is the automatic assumption of certain body postures. These range from classical yoga *asanas* (postures) to the postures of Theresa of Avila, a Christian mystic who underwent several kundalini experiences—"... convulsions, powerful enough to throw her involuntarily from her bed ... levitating ... whereby, without the use of her hands, she would spring from her knees to land standing on her head." (Irving, 1995, pp. 197-8)

During a body-centered psychotherapeutic session, I watched its awesome, physical effect on a young lawyer who came to see me. Unable to perform in the courtroom, this young lawyer was relegated to office work while his partner handled the trials. Though unhappy about the situation, his fear continued to hold him prisoner.

During an acupressure session, he experienced an incredible release of energy. As my hands cradled his head, and my fingers contacted his throat center—the center of expression—his body spontaneously arched as the back of his head and the heels of his feet became his only supports. A rapid release of powerful energy re-aligned his body and energy centers. A block had been cleared. In a short time, he was able to return to the courtroom.

As I continue to explore the mysterious reaches of the soul-body, I am aware that kundalini energy is *often* spontaneously activated, and can accelerate the psychotherapeutic process. One does not have to practice kundalini yoga to experience it; it can be activated spontaneously through bodywork and breathwork.

The highest state of consciousness (in Indian spirituality) is *ananda* or bliss. It is a grace to experience *ananda* in the physical body. I received this grace during a process acupressure treatment given to me by a colleague. As Claire worked on me, I directed my breath into my heart center and spoke of the central focus of my spiritual work, "I stay in my heart through concentration, breath and aspiration for the truth." Suddenly, I saw an image of Sai Baba, an Indian yogi, his head tilted to one side. He gazed at me with one eye. Smiling broadly, his demeanor was both playful and mischievous. I focused on his hair—a giant *Afro!* He looked like a cartoon character who had stuck his finger in an electric socket. Suddenly, this electricity flooded my body and I imagined flexible tubes channeling its flow from the top of my head through the soles of my feet. Spontaneously, my head turned to one side, Claire asked what I was experiencing:

> I am a baby, my body totally flexible, no bones—A "wrap around energy" undulates through me, and I keep rocking. I feel *bliss in my body*: I am newborn. No mind; a total awareness *in the body*. No breaks in the energy flow; the whole body is unified. Joy....

Sai Baba had given me a gift. It persisted throughout that evening and the next day.

Focusing on the mind, many psychologists have ignored the body. Focusing on realization, many spiritual seekers have also ignored it, believing it to be an obstacle on the path. Those, however, who envision an *interdependence* between body, life-force, mind and spirit believe that it is both a container for our personal history and a ground for our spiritual manifestation.

Kundalini, Trauma and Transcendence

Accessing traumatic events often opens the way to contacting the soul. Processing the journey of the physical body oftentimes reveals our personal and transpersonal history.

There are those who have suffered traumas so deep, so enigmatic, that most mental and emotional psychotherapeutic approaches are ineffective. The body itself must tell the story. Twenty-three-year-old Dustin was too traumatized to function in daily life. He suffered from severe muscle spasms and mental confusion. Engaging Dustin in conversation was challenging. He responded with a word, punctuated by silence. He squirmed, shifting as though tortured. When he spoke of his constant pain, it was without emotion.

Slowly, we unearthed some of the developmental milestones in his life. At age eighteen, he had experienced a "personality change," had become confused about sexual preference and, undergoing intense pain, had withdrawn from social contacts. His mother described him as a very happy, loving child (even through her nervous breakdown when he was three-years-old). At four, however, he attended a day camp where he was "roasted by both children and adults." Beyond verbal abuse, Dustin experienced physical and sexual abuse at this camp. His terror at this time was so great, he remembered seeing the devil.

This experience radically altered the course of Dustin's life. Once a happy, outgoing child, he became withdrawn. His terror was amplified by his father who, at times, raged uncontrollably. When left alone with him, Dustin screamed and cried until his mother returned. While his parents felt guilty for causing his condition, they also humiliated him for it.

Through process acupressure, I met another side of this paralyzed young man. Dustin's bodily signals became the pathway to his mind, emotions and spirit. When I applied pressure to the acu-points, his whole body trembled. Despite great efforts to remain motionless and silent, he grimaced constantly. Eventually, cries and shouts accompanied perpetual movement.

For one year, I worked with these explosions of energy until his iron web of contracted muscles gradually gave way to advancing energy. However, *no* memories, mental images or emotions manifested. Great mental confusion continued to exhaust him, and we were forced to trust the wisdom and power of the body's circuitry. Then, ever so slowly, the spasms diminished and Dustin was able to describe the kundalini energy's ascending route. Beginning in the sacrum, it amplified constriction in the spinal lumbar region, piercing through his abdomen into his heart. This sudden invasion evoked moans and cries as powerful jolts lifted Dustin's legs and pelvis off the table. An intense heat invaded his spine. That year, progress was measured by the energy's influx into new areas of Dustin's body. This influx advanced from sacrum to abdomen to lungs; down the arms, into the hands; towards the legs and feet. As each rusty area was released, I felt as though I was oiling the Tinman in *The Wizard of Oz*. Exhausted and confused, Dustin's mind and emotions still remained unable to integrate his bodily process.

After the first year, however, he was able to cry, express anger, verbalize his experience and recall his past. He enjoyed greater clarity of mind. But with the energy's conquest of new territories, a major blockage arose in his neck. Heavily armored, it was very sensitive to touch. He often screamed when I made contact. As I concentrated on the neck area, Dustin visualized an image, recurring throughout our work. "I see my head being chopped off." Two traumatic events emerged. The first took place at the camp he had attended when he was four. Many scenes of sitting alone arose. Then, he recalled staring at gravel; hiding in a large drain pipe; being sodomized. He relived humiliation and physical abuse. Someone stepped on his head and neck while a crowd laughed.

The image of a second traumatic event surfaced—that of a man in a hospital bed *who had broken his neck and become paralyzed*. Suddenly, he recalled his mother's repeated comment that he walked "like an old man" and his own realization of being disabled. Following the process of these synchronicities, dreams and inner experience, he re-lived a past-life as a wounded soldier, paralyzed from the neck down. The intensity of our acupressure sessions escalated. Screaming at the top of his lungs, Dustin vibrated uncontrollably. The lightest touch on his neck evoked shrieks of agony: The more he was able to receive energy and express his feelings, the more his neck released. Finally, explosions of light-energy reached his head. With this victory, a bridge was built between Dustin's head and heart. Mind and emotions began to work in concert. Bodily pain retreated. He began to study hatha yoga and meditation, slowly, gradually overcoming the effects of his trauma.

Body and Spirit

As the therapist enters the energy field of a client's fear and trauma, a dance between the two transpires. I had been working for years with a victim of ritual abuse. As our work deepened, the client re-experienced scenes of murder, rape and torture. Intensive therapy ensued and my strength ebbed.

After a session, in which terror was palpable, I returned home. Exhausted, I submerged myself in a hot bath. Afterwards, walking to the bedroom, I was inundated with a great weariness. As I fell onto the bed, I felt my life-force draining from my body. The muscles on the right side of my face and neck suddenly became flaccid, and I began to drool, uncontrollably. Fear propelled me into a sitting posture. "Was I having a stroke?" I dragged myself to the mirror and gazed querulously at the reflection. I looked normal, but could not form words to alert my partner. At last, I managed a whisper. Soon we were off to the emergency room.

I was immediately hooked up to several machines, while doctors shone lights into my eyes and stimulated different parts of my body. After four hours my speech returned. I was in the hospital overnight for observation, then referred to a neurologist. I found my mind dwelling on my client who had suffered ritual abuse. Through her history, I confronted the reality of evil in humanity and its terrifying presence in the world. I wondered if this dark, invisible presence had affected me. Had I suffered an occult attack from these hidden forces?

MRI day arrived. Warned about claustrophobia, I reclined uneasily within the machine. Though bound and unable to move in the tight chamber, I suddenly experienced a magical release. All thoughts and feelings vanished as the vision of my spiritual teacher, Sri Aurobindo, arose. As he scrutinized the right side of my face with his steady gaze, I felt an inexplicable radiance. I enjoyed his divine Presence for the entire time I was in the machine, even experiencing his fragrance (rose petals and sandalwood).

Several days later, I met with the neurologist. There were absolutely no signs of physical impairment! When I asked him why this had happened, he replied simply, "Sometimes we just don't know."

*   *   *   *

Limited by the perceptions of the sensory mind, the body at first appears dense and impermeable. However, in actuality, it reveals untold pathways between this solid frame and more subtle levels of our being. Somatic therapists agree that direct access to the mind and the emotions can be gained through touch:

> There is a substantial difference between approaching the psyche through touch and approaching the psyche through talk. Much of what may take several sessions of therapeutic dialogue to achieve often can be done in a few moments using touch. (Ford, 1989, p. 122)

While there is a growing consensus that the body can be used as a vehicle to the mind and the emotions, this is not the final frontier. A spiritual energy—*kundalini*—of even higher vibrational frequency than mind or emotions can arise within the body. This kundalini force has the power to unveil both subconscious (trauma) and superconscious (past life recall) formations. Since the body can help us access the furthest reaches of consciousness, the body of psychological thought must evolve if it is to incorporate this relatively new frontier. Body, mind and emotions must inevitably be joined by a fourth force—spirit, if the whole being is to be healed.

In the following chapter, we will explore the interdependence of body, mind, emotions and spirit in formulating an *integral psychology*.

CHAPTER

3

A Soul-Centered Psychology

... the ego is the individual only in the ignorance; there is a true
individual who is not the ego and still has an eternal relation
with all other individuals which is not egoistic or self-separative,
but of which the essential character is practical mutuality
founded on essential unity. (Sri Aurobindo, 1987, p. 372)

WESTERN PSYCHOLOGY has focused its efforts on preserving and
strengthening the ego. Identified with this ego, confined by
ordinary consciousness, we rarely experience a greater reality.
However, disruption of ordinary consciousness can and does
occur. Sometimes uninvited, expanded awareness may follow as
a result of abuse or loss. Occasionally, it even manifests spontaneously.

One night several years ago in a high school gymnasium in
Massachusetts, I experienced a spontaneous disruption of ordinary consciousness.

Standing on a seemingly endless line in a gymnasium transformed by images of India, I was slowly led to Ammachi, a small
Indian woman with a jet-black braid. Greeting each with a smile,
she drew us, in turn, into a loving embrace, stroking each back,
whispering into each ear. Suddenly, I found myself kneeling
before her. As I wondered how such a tiny woman could embrace
such a tall man, I suddenly found myself in her arms. Free-falling

42

into the gentle folds of her white sari, I heard her chant, "Ma, Ma, Ma, Ma...." As her hand moved up and down my spine, my chaotic mental dance abruptly ceased. For several moments I was released from my mind's prison. The people and the room disappeared. I had no thought of before or after. Only a vast eternal and loving Now.

Ammachi grasped my shoulders. Gazing through my eyes into my soul, she applied sandalwood paste to the center of my forehead, then released me with the invocation, *Jai Ma* (victory to the Mother).

Attendants helped me to my feet. Turning, I beheld hundreds of smiling faces—but from a new perspective. My inner *and* outer perception had been radically altered. A column of conscious energy witnessed the myriad images about me. It processed my mental patterns and I experienced thoughts, emotions and bodily sensations as if they were projected on a screen. From this new center, "I" was *aware* of all the movements of my being, but *was not identified* with them.

Watching a movie, I sometimes find myself immersed in the story projected on the screen. Momentarily, I become aware of myself as a witness. Contact with Ammachi threw me into just such a *still point*. Unmoved by passing thoughts and feelings, "I" now identified with the *soul*.

Later, as I walked through the gym studying photos of Ammachi, "I" watched the mental battle: "How long will this altered state of consciousness last? I don't want to lose it! But I'm not even a disciple of Ammachi! Why do I experience myself as taller?"

For the moment, I inhabited a body of higher vibrational frequency—a *new* body. The four-hour drive home seemed a matter of minutes. A dense, solid energy flowed steadily. While this "new" body's energetic edges lay *beyond* the physical body, I experienced it *behind* the personality. Mind, emotions and body became extensions of a central being. In ordinary consciousness

"I" am my body, my ideas, my feelings. In extra-ordinary consciousness, my center of awareness shifts; I identify with my soul
and experience life *from inside out.*

The soul reflected a new reality and for the next two days I
lived in this quiet joy marveling at the juxtaposition of soul and
personality. I asked myself, "How can the calm focus of the soul
co-exist with the chaotic flux of the personality? Can the personality be guided to *reveal* rather than *veil* the soul?"

*Our exploration of a soul-centered psychology will emphasize
not only the transformative power of the soul but also the longing
of this center of our true individuality to fully manifest in our
personality.*

The Surface Personality

The ego is a psychic structure that is based on crystallized beliefs
about who we are and what the world is. We experience
ourselves and the world through the filter of this structure.
(Almaas, 2000, pp. 21-22)

The central belief of personality is: *"I" am separate from
every other person.* Jettisoned from the sense of oneness in the
womb, this alienation evolves slowly. Since the infant does not
know where he ends and his mother begins, a symbiotic unity
predominates. Under favorable conditions, the newborn experiences unity: There is no sense of separation from the mother.
However, this unity is soon lost. As the infant grows, he begins to
feel separate and alone. As this sense of unity crumbles, he
discovers psychological mechanisms of identification and projection in order to gain acceptance.

Most psychologists feel that this sense of separation is directly
proportional to the growth of the ego-personality, that "normal"
psychological development is synonymous with ego-boundary.
The therapeutic goal: An integrated personality with a strong
sense of I-ness as the center—the clearing-house for all thoughts,

feelings and actions. Without this center one experiences some degree of depersonalization. Balancing the inner pressures of the unconscious, and the outer pressures of the world, it is believed that this center, this *fragile fulcrum*, leads us to our sense of self. It is perceived as our *only* center and the focal point of most psychotherapeutic endeavor.

A psychology perceiving soul as the center of our being must re-evaluate all concepts of personality and self, whether normal or abnormal.

How can we become aware of this deeper center? What can become the impetus, the catalyst, for this realization? Our first sense of individuality arises from a false consciousness of separation from other beings. While this ego-sense provides a center for functioning in the world, it can also engender a feeling of suffocation: Fear and contraction, hallmarks of ego consciousness, create a prison until separation becomes unbearable.

Crisis—an illness, a loss, a betrayal, a death can move us to a deeper search for meaning and unity. Crisis causes a disruption of identification with the temporary self. This disruption creates a crack in the personality which can initiate the search for soul.

Our search for meaning and unity may also be triggered by a star-filled sky, a poem, a song, the touch of a spiritual teacher. The boundary between subject and object disappears and there arises the joy of identification with something greater than the ego-bound self.

> Even in the littleness of our mortal state,
> Even in this prison-house of outer form,
> A brilliant passage for the infallible Flame
> Is driven through gross walls of nerve and brain,
> A Splendor presses or a power breaks through,
> Earth's great dull barrier is removed awhile,
> The inconscient seal is lifted from our eyes
> And we grow vessels of creative might.
> (Sri Aurobindo, 1996, p. 108)

The claustrophobia of the ego-center and the influx of the authentic self are necessary companions. However, without a signal from the latter, we might never gain the trust and courage to relinquish the ego's death-grip. Even when the time arrives to journey between these two companions, we find the passage populated with "demons," as well as "angels." We fear separation from familiar mental grooves. We fear the unfamiliar expansiveness of consciousness. Faced with this dual fear, we must choose.

A Paradigm Shift

Sri Aurobindo's exposition of our psycho-spiritual make-up stands in sharp contrast to that of Western psychology.

> ... the truth is that all this that is behind, this sea of which our waking consciousness is only a wave or series of waves, cannot be described by any one term, for it is very complex. Part of it is subconscient, lower than waking consciousness; part of it is on a level with it but behind and much larger than it; part of it is above and superconscient to us. (Sri Aurobindo, 1995, pp. 348-9)

Before the advent of psychoanalysis, psychology had developed as a laboratory science studying aspects of behavior bordering on physiology. Sigmund Freud's discovery of the unconscious (with its predominant role in determining behavior) set the stage for self-examination in modern Western psychology. Unlike Sri Aurobindo, however, he offered a *circumscribed* paradigm of the reality behind our waking consciousness.

Through his study of psycho-pathology, Freud began to perceive the unconscious as a mental domain containing repressed images, desires, memories, etc. Although not normally accessible to the conscious mind, they play a powerful role in determining human behavior. Employing a variety of introspective approaches (recovery of repressed memories through hypnosis, dream analysis, free association) in order to gain access to the unconscious, he formulated a "topographical" theory of mind composed of three layers—conscious, preconscious (ordinary forgetting), unconscious (repressed forgetting), followed by a "structural" theory of personality:

1. Id—primitive instinctual energies.
2. Ego—thinking part of mind (perception, memory, problem solving).
3. Superego—conscience for the ego, censoring instinctual demands of id.

Calling the id the true unconscious, Freud admitted that much of the ego and superego were also unconscious.

Carl Jung, one of Freud's early collaborators, discovered another dimension of the unconscious, a collective level beyond the personal. He claimed that the personal unconscious contains long-forgotten events, subliminal impressions and buried psychic knowledge—thus disagreeing with Freud who claimed that it contained only repressed memories. The collective unconscious is composed of universal human instincts born of millions of years of ancestral experience. This collective experience has created deep psychic pre-dispositions in the entire human race, powerful primordial images (*archetypes*) found universally in dreams, fantasies, fairy tales, myths *and* the "delusions" of psychotics. These archetypes include Mother, Father, Self, Child, Wise Old Man, Great Mother.

Jung's discovery of the collective unconscious opened the way to a transpersonal psychology—a psychology based on the belief that instincts and archetypes were paramount in the unconscious. In the conscious mind, instinct operates as the impulse of self-preservation, self-procreation; and archetypes as universal ideas. For Freud this instinct was primarily sexual. Though he extended his vision to include the life instinct (Eros), and the death instinct (Thanatos), in practice psychoanalysis reduces all aspiration and creativity to the sexual urge—whereas Jung, pioneer of the transpersonal, regards the libido as a *psychic energy,* one which manifests in many forms (including the sexual)—but primarily as spiritual energy (numinosity).

Though Freud's thinking on mind and personality no longer dominates, his concept of the unconscious is still a touchstone for many contemporary psychologists. While Jung's theory of the collective unconscious has gained more acceptance, this acceptance is limited. Some psychologists feel that Jung's preoccupation with religion, archetypes and the soul have placed him on the *fringe* of mainstream psychology. However, Marion Woodman reminds them

> Psychology means the science of the soul. The terrible irony is that many psychologists think of themselves as scientists who do not believe there is such a thing as the soul. (Woodman, 1993, p. 40)

We arrive now at a crossroads in the evolution of psychological thought. On one road we encounter Freud's *and* Jung's claim that in the juxtaposition of the unconscious and egoic consciousness, consciousness is unconditionally identified with the development of a strong ego. Neither acknowledge a state of consciousness in which ego is transcended or eradicated. For Jung "consciousness is inconceivable without an ego.... If there is no ego, there is nobody to be conscious of anything." (cited in Dalal, 1991, p. 19) Despite his contact with Eastern thought, and his acknowledgment of a Self beyond ego, he did not envision *total* identification with the Self.

We encounter identification with the Self in the *ancient, perennial psychology* found in Buddhism, Christianity, Hinduism, Taoism and Sufism, as well as in contemporary Transpersonal Psychology. This psychology claims *a poise of consciousness transcending the egoic, and radically transforming our awareness of self, and our relationship with others and the world. Separation* is replaced by *unity,* and experiences transcending the ordinary states of consciousness (unitive, cosmic, awakening of kundalini, clairvoyance, clairaudience, telekinesis, visionary, past-life) are no longer relegated to a fringe area of psychology, or reduced to the "unconscious strivings of the id." While Freud's and Jung's investigations of the relationship between the unconscious and the conscious mind were ground-breaking, *we now need to explore a new paradigm which fully recognizes states of consciousness transcending ego and personality.*

Jung recognized the limitations inherent in recognizing the unconscious:

> Science employs the term "the unconscious," thus admitting that it knows nothing about it, for it can know nothing about the substance of the psyche when the sole means of knowing anything is the psyche. (Jung, 1989, p. 310)

To map "the unconscious," we must pierce the walls separating our egoic consciousness from levels of consciousness behind and beyond it.

> ... it is only by going inward behind the veil of superficial mind and living within, in an inner mind, an inner life, an inmost soul of our being that we can be fully self-aware,—by this and by rising to a higher plane of mind than that which our waking consciousness inhabits. An enlargement and completion of our present evolutionary status ... would be the result of such an inward living; but an evolution beyond it can come only by one becoming conscious in what is now superconscient to us, by an ascension to the native heights of Spirit. (Sri Aurobindo, 1987, p. 736)

Be it "the unconscious" of modern depth psychology, or "the inner being" of Sri Aurobindo's Integral Yoga, the critical question for the evolution of psychology and consciousness is: How can we *know* the reality that lies beyond our present mental consciousness? Both Jung and Sri Aurobindo agree that the mind is not equipped to accomplish this task. But unlike the latter, Jung persisted in identifying individual existence with egoic, rather than soul consciousness.

> Since the Unconscious really means the not-conscious, nobody can gain that state while he is alive, and be able to remember it afterwards, as the Hindus claim. (cited in Serrano, 1968, p. 49)

Again, unlike Sri Aurobindo, he believed the superconscious to be "...a metaphysical concept and as a consequence outside my interests. I wish to proceed solely on facts and experience." (Serrano, p. 50) The main focus of his work was to establish a dialogue between the ego and the unconscious, ego being intimately related to individuality and consciousness.

> So far, I have found no stable or definite centre in the unconscious and I don't believe such a centre exists. I believe that the thing which I call the Self is an ideal centre, equidistant between the Ego and the Unconscious, and it is probably equivalent to the maximum natural expression of individuality, in a state of fulfillment or totality. As nature aspires to express itself, so does man, and the Self is that dream of totality. It is therefore an ideal centre, something created. (Serrano, p. 49)

Jung's beliefs reflect the difference between the depth psychology of the West and the yoga psychology of the East.

The Involution and Evolution of Consciousness

Search for a soul-centered psychology leads us beyond egoic individuality to the individuality of the soul. The ego will disappear, and with it the experience of *individuality as separation*. Sri Aurobindo further unveils this basic difference by describing the five dimensions of consciousness—*the surface or frontal being, the subconscient, the subliminal, the psychic being, the super-conscient.*

Since the human being is a microcosm of the universe, our evolution reflects that of nature. Consciousness is not an epiphenomenon of our organs. It does not mysteriously evolve from a blind, driven unconsciousness.

> Consciousness is a fundamental thing ... in existence—it is the energy, ... the movement of consciousness that creates the universe and all that is in it—not only the macrocosm but the microcosm is nothing but consciousness arranging itself. (Sri Aurobindo, 1995, p. 236)

This self-aware force of existence was there before the creation of the universe. The undifferentiated Oneness of the Infinite created, through a process of Self-limitation, the multiplicity of forms. Unlike the Western concept, that creation arises from *nothing*, Sri Aurobindo proceeds from the (self-evident) principle that nothing itself exists *outside of infinity*. Finite creation evolves *within* infinity—through limitation.

This creative process of Self-limitation, *involution*, conceals the force of consciousness (*cit-sakti*), through a multiplicity of finite forms. This descent of consciousness reaches its most involved forms in Matter, and through the process of evolution returns to its highest expression in Spirit.

Seven gradations of being and consciousness manifest in this involutionary and evolutionary process. The first three represent the expression of the Divine as *Sachchidananda*: Existence (*Sat*), Consciousness (*Chit-sakti*), Bliss (*Ananda*). These three universal states of consciousness constitute the essential nature of the Divine. Rising into this upper hemisphere, we enter Oneness, leaving the worlds of multiplicity behind.

A fourth gradation, the supramental Truth-Consciousness, is the power of self-determination of the Infinite. It has the capacity to manifest unity in infinite multiplicity, thereby integrating the upper and lower hemispheres. Within this quadruple power of the upper hemisphere there is full expression of knowledge and freedom.

The remaining three powers, of Mind, Life and Matter, are limited powers that are still separated from their source. Multiplicity and separation dominate our consciousness in this lower hemisphere.

> ... this separation creates a state of limited knowledge exclusively concentrated on its own limited world-order and oblivious of all that is behind it and of the underlying unity, a state of ... cosmic and individual Ignorance. (Sri Aurobindo, 1987, p. 663)

The involutionary descent of consciousness culminates in a plane *devoid of* consciousness. Sri Aurobindo calls it the Inconscient. Paradoxically, it is the very starting point of the evolutionary return of consciousness to its Source.

> ... this One Being and Consciousness is involved here in Matter. Evolution is the method by which it liberates itself; Consciousness appears in what seems to be inconscient, and once having appeared is self-impelled to grow higher and higher and at the same time to enlarge and develop towards a greater and greater perfection. Life is the first step of this release of consciousness; mind is the second; but the evolution does not finish with mind, it awaits a release into something greater, a Consciousness which is spiritual and supramental. (Sri Aurobindo, 2000, p. 95)

This macrocosmic descent and ascent of Being and Consciousness is replicated in the psycho-spiritual process of each human being. As microcosms, we possess all of the transcendent and universal levels of consciousness. We exist as transitional beings on the evolutionary ladder. Just as the animal was a laboratory for working out the appearance of the human, so the human is a laboratory for working out the emergence of the supramental being. Our capacity for self-consciousness places us in the unique position to hasten our individual as well as universal evolution. Empowered by this evolutionary vision, we can now examine Sri Aurobindo's formulation of "a greater psychology."

Paradigm for an Integrated Consciousness

> ... you must know the whole before you can know the part and the highest before you can truly understand the lowest. That is the promise of the greater psychology awaiting its hour.... (Sri Aurobindo, 1995, p. 1609)

This "greater psychology" will embrace *all* experiences of the body, life-force, mind, soul and spirit. A full spectrum psychology will understand cosmic consciousness as a way of knowing common to mystics of both East and West, no longer interpreting it as the workings of a dysfunctional mind in need of medication. Ignorance of these deeper realms of consciousness can cause great suffering.

Gaining Access to the Inner Being

Sri Aurobindo often refers to the subliminal as the "psychical consciousness," what Indian psychology calls the "subtle" or "dream self." This consciousness possesses the power to see, through psychical sense images, all things in time and space— past, present or future. An expanded consciousness, it is, however, also limited. "As exercised by clairvoyants, mediums and others this is ... a specialized faculty limited though often precise and accurate in action, and implies no development of the inner soul or the spiritual being or the higher intelligence." (Sri Aurobindo, 1992, p. 862) Whether opened by chance or an innate gift, the subliminal begins to transmit images (visual, auditory, proprioceptive) from the universal mind. If there is no interpretation of these images from the egoic mind, a true transcription can be received.

Patricia was an alcoholic who used intoxicants to drown the voices in her head. In her early thirties, this mother of two began hearing voices—often full conversations. She feared that she was "going crazy." Alone in her room, she actually "heard" a conversation between her best friend and her son who were miles away. Slowly, she realized that she was "hearing" on an extra-ordinary level. Her perception of herself and reality shifted as she confirmed the content of their conversation. With this new understanding, she began her search for the psychic experience. As she developed her gift, her need for alcohol receded.

Patricia's crisis reveals an opening between her *surface* and *subliminal* consciousness. In Sri Aurobindo's terms, surface being is waking consciousness. Composed selectively of mind, life-force (vital) and matter (body), this mix, organized around the ego, constitutes the outer personality. On this level of consciousness, Patricia's ordinary way of perceiving reality was through the sensory, conditioned mind which limits communication to the boundaries of the senses. Most psychologists, analyzing on this egoic level, would evaluate Patricia's experience as pathological and would eliminate her auditory "hallucinations" through medication.

The clash of two different "beings" within her created a crisis for Patricia. What was the nature of this disrupting consciousness? The answer could be found only in the existence of the *subliminal* being. Sri Aurobindo describes the subliminal as a consciousness that is greater, wider, more luminous than waking consciousness.

> The subliminal self stands behind and supports the whole superficial man; it has a larger and more efficient mind behind the surface mind, a larger and more powerful vital behind the surface vital, a subtler and freer physical consciousness behind the surface bodily existence. And above them it opens to higher

superconscient as well as below them to lower subconscient ranges. (Sri Aurobindo, 1995, p. 1606)

Crossing the border between the surface and the subliminal being is like entering a foreign land. One leaves the world of separation and indirect experience and enters a realm where direct contact with a universal consciousness is common. We enter this "larger room" in our being when we sleep and receive the transcript of our time there through dream images. Trance states, hypnosis, meditation and spontaneous openings like Patricia's can also give us access to the subliminal.

Hypnotism encourages the waking mind to sleep or to enter a trance state. This liberates the subliminal (or true) mind, a mind free from the constraints of the body. Hence, during trance-induction, the inner mental being (master of the nervous system) can, for example, receive suggestions to feel no pain during dental work or childbirth.

Gaining access to the inner being through sleep, concentration or trance opens the being to *three fields of consciousness*:

a) The *subconscious* from which repressed memories can be recovered.

b) The *subliminal* which allows a more direct and universal way of knowing—through occult powers, clairvoyance, clairaudience, transference of thought, telepathy.

c) The *superconscious* where all mental or sensory experience ceases—the experience of "God," "Spirit," "Over-soul."

The notion that subliminal realms can be accessed in trance states became clear to me during my participation in an experiment conducted by Jean Houston. Guided into trance, waking consciousness ceased and I entered subliminal realms. In this state, I walked along a road in a barren landscape and came upon a gated city. Entering, I went directly to its center, a gigantic marble fountain. To the left of this fountain stood a man with long white beard and hair. He wore the traditional Indian *dhoti* (a white cloth wrapped around the body with the end draped over one shoulder). Silently, he directed me into the fountain. The fountain's column of water became the rising energy in my spine (kundalini).

Later I realized I had received spiritual initiation from Sri Aurobindo: Entering subliminal realms, I had been touched by the superconscious.

> The subliminal has the right of entry into the mental, and vital and subtle physical planes of the universal consciousness. It is not confined to the material plane and the physical world; it possesses means of communication with the worlds of being which the descent towards involution created in its passage and with all corresponding planes or worlds that may have arisen or been constructed to serve the purpose of re-ascent from Inconscience to Superconscience. (Sri Aurobindo, 1987, p. 426)

In part, the subliminal corresponds to Jung's *collective unconscious*, that realm of psyche distinct from the *personal unconscious*, containing the inherited experiences of the human race: the *archetypes*—universal ideas, images that transcend particular cultural expressions (Wise Old Man, Child, Mother). For Sri Aurobindo,

> It [the subliminal] is according to our psychology, connected with the small outer personality by certain centres of consciousness (chakras) of which we become aware by yoga. Only a little of the inner being escapes through these centres into the outer life, but that little is the best part of ourselves and responsible for our art, poetry, philosophy, ideals, religious aspirations, efforts at knowledge and perfection. (Sri Aurobindo, 1995, pp. 1164-65)

The Subconscious Being

Modern depth psychology characterizes all psychic phenomena beyond waking consciousness as *unconscious*. Sri Aurobindo, however, describes a greater reality: *It is the surface personality which is unconscious of the inner consciousness.* But within this inner consciousness he delineates the *subconscious* from the *subliminal*. Unlike the subliminal which is wider, more luminous than waking consciousness, the subconscious is "... an obscure unconsciousness or half-consciousness ... in a way inferior to and less than our organized waking awareness..." (Sri Aurobindo, 1987, p. 557). Except for transpersonal psychology, modern psychology has focused its attention primarily on the subconscious, prompting Sri Aurobindo to say,

> Modern psychology is an infant science, at once rash, fumbling and crude. As in all infant sciences, the universal habit of the human mind—to take a partial or local truth, generalize it unduly and try to explain a whole field of Nature in its narrow terms—runs riot here. (Sri Aurobindo, 1995, p. 1606)

He charges Freudian psychoanalysis with exaggerating the importance of suppressed sexual complexes, while mistaking a "few ill-lit corners" of the lower vital subconscious for the subliminal whole. As a great yogi, Sri Aurobindo's personal transcendence of egoic consciousness endowed him with intimate knowledge of the "inner being." Freud and Jung knew this realm of the inner being solely through the filter of the ego. That part of the psyche they called *unconscious* is actually composed of *varying levels of consciousness. The future of psychology lies in free exploration of this inner being, unhampered by pathological paradigms of the psyche.*

Modern psychology's preoccupation with the subconscious is quite understandable given its nature. A partial list of subconscious material includes: bad habits of the body which cause us to fall ill; past impressions, associations, fixed notions and nervous reactions. One can also include all suppressed or repressed experiences that were overwhelming—what psychology calls "complexes." This material can suddenly rise into consciousness at anytime through dream, or mechanical repetitions of thought, emotions, sensations or action.

> The subconscient is the main cause why all things repeat themselves and nothing ever gets changed except in appearance. It is the cause why people say character cannot be changed, ... it is the main support of death and disease.... (Sri Aurobindo, 1995, p. 355)

The repetitive, cyclical nature of the subconscious explains somewhat the exceedingly slow pace of psychotherapy. Great investments of time, energy and money are expended, while the return is often meager; ego psychology possesses neither the knowledge nor the power to effect the cyclical nature of the subconscious. In contrast, Sri Aurobindo's psychology directly accesses the psychic being, the subliminal and the super-conscious, thus effecting a speedier change and transformation.

Unlike the yogas of ascension which leave human nature unchanged, Sri Aurobindo's yoga harnesses higher levels of consciousness in order to oust the seemingly intractable problem of the subconscious. Although we might prefer to ignore this bed of quicksand, the Mother (Sri Aurobindo's spiritual partner) unveils our true work.

> We are disgusted with the world as it is—and we have the POWER to change it. But we are such fools that we can't bring ourselves to abdicate our silly, little personality to let the Marvel unfold. And that's all accumulated in the sub-conscient: every-thing we have rejected is there, and now it must be brought in contact with the transforming force ... so that this unconscious-ness may come to an end. (Mother, 1951-1973, Vol. 13, pp. 227-8)

At this juncture, Sri Aurobindo's Integral Yoga joins modern depth psychology in the herculean task of making the unconscious conscious. Recognizing the impotence of ego, it offers modern psychology the power of the soul, the subliminal and the superconscious. Unless it embraces these powers, it will continue to cycle in its subconscious swamp.

The Psychic Being

Enshrouded in the confines of our personality, we eventually discover our authentic center, the evolving soul. This feminine aspect of the Divine, the Shakti or Divine Mother, embodies herself in each human being.

> But since she knows the toil of mind and life,
> As a mother feels and shares her children's lives,
> She puts forth a small portion of herself,
> A being no bigger than the thumb of man
> Into a hidden region of the heart
> To face the pang and forget the bliss,
> To share the suffering and endure life's wounds
> And labour mid the labour of the stars.
> This in us laughs and weeps, suffers the stroke,
> Exults in victory, struggles for the crown,
> Identified with the mind and body and life,
> It takes on itself their anguish and defeat,
> Bleeds with Fate's whips and hangs upon the cross,
> Yet is the unwounded and immortal self
> Supporting the actor on the human scene.
> (Sri Aurobindo, 1996, pp. 526-27)

Sri Aurobindo claims that our human suffering is shared by a small portion of the divine self, placed in "a hidden region of the heart." Though limited by mind, body and life, it remains, paradoxically, the "unwounded and immortal self." Our quest for a greater psychology must eventually lead us to the awakening of this self, this psychic being—to a shift from ego to soul as the center of our being. The route itself, as well as the very moments of awakening, create the most meaningful story of our life. Its common threads are:

1. Amplification of embodied experience of mind, body and vital.
2. Habitation of a body larger than the physical.
3. Powerful feelings of joy, love, ecstasy.
4. Overwhelming sensations in the area of the heart.
5. Growing consciousness of soul being *behind* the personality.
6. Equanimity in times of stress.

Sri Aurobindo's adventure of consciousness guides us beyond the confines of the surface personality, through the subliminal worlds of inner mind, vital and physical to the *inmost being—the psychic being*—the *embodied* part of the soul, which supports both the inner and the surface being. He then distinguishes between three forms of this being: The Jivatman, the spark soul and the psychic being.

The *Jivatman* is the eternal, true being of the individual. It exists above the manifest instrument (mind, life, body and psychic being) and does not pass through birth or death. This portion of the Divine Self, sometimes called *atman, self or spirit*, supports the evolving being but is not limited by it.

The *Spark Soul* is the Divine spark which descends into the material creation to support its evolution. It contains all evolutionary possibilities and is present in all living beings.

The *Psychic Being* is the evolving soul

> ... that comes down into birth and passes through death— although it does not itself die, for it is immortal—from one state to another, from the earth plane to other planes and back again to the earth-existence. It goes on with this progression from life

to life through an evolution which leads it up to the human state and evolves through it all a being of itself which we call the psychic being that supports the evolution and develops a physical, a vital, a mental human consciousness as its instruments of world experience and of a disguised, imperfect, but growing self-expression. (Sri Aurobindo, 1995, pp. 438-39)

This self-expression is eternally supported by the presence of soul. The spark soul resides first in material objects, then through evolution in the vital world of plant and animal. Having acquired this life-force, soul awaits the next evolutionary step. With the advent of mind, interaction with the material and vital planes then produces the human being. At this evolutionary juncture the soul discovers an even higher degree of expression, evolution of a *soul-personality—a divine individuality.*

The psychic being grows along with the mental, vital and physical bodies. In its undeveloped state, it is veiled or totally dominated by its own instruments. Ego reigns and is identified with some combination of the mental, vital and physical; but the life of this being has not yet become conscious of the divine within.

As the psychic being evolves it becomes more dominant, influencing the mental, vital and physical and even creating certain *psychic openings.* As Sri Aurobindo metaphorically relates in his epic poem, *Savitri,* "Unknown to himself lives a hidden king, behind rich tapestries in great secret rooms." (Sri Aurobindo, 1996, p. 479) Led to a spiritual path, the mental, vital and physical bodies begin to *consciously* call forth the psychic being—the hidden king. This step hastens the evolutionary process of soul, replacing ego as the center of our being.

How are we to recognize the psychic being? What are its characteristics?

The psychic is not above but *behind*—its seat is behind the heart, its power is not knowledge but an essential or spiritual feeling— it has the clearest sense of the Truth and a sort of inherent perception of it which is of the nature of soul-perception and soul-feeling. (Sri Aurobindo, 1995, pp. 268-69)

The psychic being gives us a sense of *the good, the beautiful, the true.* "It is the concealed Witness and Control, the hidden Guide, the Daemon of Socrates, the inner light or voice of the mystic." (Sri Aurobindo, 1987, p. 225) Although immortal, during each lifetime this traveler, like the chick in the egg, must continue to peck at the coverings of conditioning. One day, however, the tough shell cracks, at last, under the pressure of its expanding inhabitant.

> ... a time comes when it is able to prepare to come out from behind the veil, to take command and turn all the instrumental nature towards a divine fulfillment. This is the beginning of the true spiritual life. (Sri Aurobindo, 1995, pp. 438-39)

Two roads open in this journey of the soul. 1) Identification with the *unembodied* Jivatman (in its unity with the transcendent and universal) eventually leads to *liberation* from material life. 2) Identification with the *embodied* psychic being eventually leads to *transformation* of material life. However, "... for the *transformation* of the life and nature the awakening of the psychic being and its rule over the nature are indispensable." (Sri Aurobindo, 1995, pp. 282-83)

The integral yoga psychology of Sri Aurobindo and the Mother bridges the schism between modern depth psychology and traditional spirituality which seeks liberation by escaping the world, the body and the subconscious. Unable to envision consciousness without an ego, modern depth psychology aborts the journey to the true center of our being; while too often traditional spirituality abandons human nature, judging it as unchangeable. Awareness of the psychic being then becomes the stepping stone in crossing the subconscious toward conscious transformation.

Psychic transformation is that evolutionary moment when the embodied soul attains the *degree of individuation* necessary to make it leader of the evolving being. With the emergence of this new center, there is no longer the need for ego.

> The soul is able now to make itself ready for a higher evolu-
> tion of manifested consciousness than the mental human—it
> can pass from the mental to the spiritual and through degrees
> of the spiritual to the supramental state. (Sri Aurobindo, 1995,
> p. 439)

Though Sri Aurobindo speaks of a triple transformation of consciousness, only the link between modern depth psychology and yoga psychology will be discussed. The correlation between modern depth psychology and yoga psychology depicts the movement of the surface being towards the center of the inner being—*the embodied soul*, constituting the true individuality of which mind, emotions and body are merely instruments. This psychological organization of the being presents a radical challenge to Western psychology and its theories of personality development:

> The psychic entity within ... the spiritual individual in us, is the
> Person that we are; but the "I" of this moment, the "I" of this life
> is only a formation, a temporary personality of this inner
> Person.... (Sri Aurobindo, 1987, p. 821)

(The remaining two transformations—*spiritualisation* and *supramentalisation*—comprise what Sri Aurobindo calls the *superconscious being*. These higher levels of consciousness will ultimately descend into the embodied being, thus birthing the next evolutionary species.)

Egoic and Soul Individuality

Sri Aurobindo's mapping of the human psyche reveals parallel processes of individuation. The surface being develops by organizing its experiences of the external and internal worlds around the ego—the temporary individual. The psychic being harnesses experiences of mind, life and body from lifetime to lifetime in order to individuate and emerge as the true individual.

What is the relationship between these two parallel processes?

Modern psychology sets its sights on the development of a strong ego/individuality. Our experience of a "self" more or less unified is the touchstone of our existence: "Myself" and "I" are used interchangeably, establishing an identity between ego and self. *I feel, I think, I act* thus becomes the center from which we engage both the external and the internal worlds. Nevertheless, cast in this herculean role this "self/ego" often feels fragile and inadequate.

Self/ego defines itself by a process of establishing boundaries which separate it from everyone and everything (not-self). In Western psychology this process is considered as normal psychological development: The sense of individuality is then dependent on the *separateness* between self and others. Without this sense of self, "I" would dissolve into an amorphous mass of thought, feelings, bodily sensations. This dissolution often leads to depersonalization and a variety of psychiatric disorders.

Sri Aurobindo's and Mother's yoga psychology acknowledges the necessity of the ego—but as a *provisional* self/individuality. In this psychology it is simply *formative*: One must become an authentic individual before the ego can relinquish its role.

> First one must become a conscious, well-knit, *individualised* being, who exists in himself, independently of all his surroundings, who can hear anything, read anything, see anything without changing. He receives from outside only what he wants to receive; he automatically refuses all that is not in conformity with his plan and nothing can leave an imprint on him unless he agrees to receive the imprint. (Mother, 1972-1987, 6:257)

The *individualisation* reaches far beyond the expectation of normal ego development. Yet even in this phase of "becoming," one can awaken to the need to transcend the fixed notion of *separation*. A person imprisoned by "individuality," ... "may suddenly have the experience of contact with his psychic which opens all the doors.... They may close again later, but once they have opened you never forget it." (Mother, 1972-1987, 6:334)

As the two centers (ego and psychic being) co-exist, two lines of individuation unfold. In the first phase one is totally identified with ego and its work of erecting ego boundaries. In the second phase while ego remains the primary center, soul manifests periodically. We begin at last to *witness* the ego thus initiating a process of dis-identification. Eventually, the psychic being *fully* emerges and becomes master of the entire being. This *psychic transformation* establishes permanent contact with our *true individuality*.

Without conscious contact with the psychic being we identify with different combinations of mind, body and vital: These identifications reflect different, discordant personalities. Unless our goal is liberation beyond the embodied being, they must be organized around the psychic being. Sri Aurobindo calls this process

—integration, the harmonisation of the being. That cannot be done from outside, it cannot be done by mind and vital being— they are sure to bungle their affair. It can be done only from within by the soul, the Spirit which is the centraliser,... (Sri Aurobindo, 1995, p. 53)

Harmonization requires total surrender of the ego. It must fully empower the soul as the central agent, harmonizing the many parts of our being for one must become individuated before the need for ego will disappear. Thus, even before the psychic being becomes fully realized, *the work of individuation can develop.* What is the work of individuation? What does it mean to be completely individualized?

> We are made up of many different parts which have to be unified around the psychic being, if we are conscious of it or at least around the central aspiration. If this unification is not done, we carry this division within us. To do this Each thought, each feeling, each sensation, each impulse, each reaction, as it manifests, must be presented in the consciousness to the central being or its aspiration. What is in accord is accepted; what is not in accord is refused, rejected or transformed. (Mother, 1972-1987, 16:362-63)

Becoming an individual means becoming a conscious, independent being differentiated from the amorphous mass. Individualization requires thorough self-inquiry— "Which thoughts come from me? Which thoughts come from others? Why am I feeling this way? Why am I in this mood?"

> You are to be conscious of yourself, you must awake to the nature and movements, you must know why and how you do things or feel or think them; you must understand your motives and impulses, the forces hidden and apparent that move you; in fact, you must ... take to pieces the entire machinery of your being. (Mother, 1972-1987, 3:1-2)

The Convergence of Integral Yoga Psychology and Psychotherapy

Sri Aurobindo's and Mother's Integral Yoga differs radically from Western psychotherapy. The former envisions integration and transformation of the entire being—body, mind, vital, soul and spirit. The latter strives to change behavior, develop personality, become aware. *The common ground is the process of becoming conscious.*

In the second phase of individuation (in which ego and psychic being both co-exist), consciousness of all parts of the being becomes *synonymous* with individuation. The central focus of the integrated psychotherapies (Mindell, Raheem, Grof) is the same. While the Mother's directive, "..*x* you must ... take to pieces the entire machinery of your being" is more radical than the goals of these therapies, both yoga psychology and integrated psychotherapies are uncovering a psychology of consciousness in which we are no longer harnessed to a "medical model" of psychological exploration which is dependent on the functioning of the material realm and those ego states of consciousness deemed "normal." On the contrary, they free us to explore states of consciousness that are both universal and transcendent. Discovery of hidden parts of our being, parts that must eventually be integrated into the *conscious* life of the individual, is one of the main goals of the integrated psychotherapies.

Spiritual paths that seek escape from the personality and the subconscious, differ significantly from Integral Yoga. The latter focuses the power of spiritual consciousness on *all* parts of the being, including the subconscious,

> One is born with a slough to clean before one begins to live. And once you have made a good start on the way to the inner transformation and you go down to the sub-conscient root of the being—that exactly which comes from parents, from atavism—...almost all difficulties are there, there are very few things added to existence after the first years of life. (Mother, 1972-1987, 4:261)

This cleaning process advances through consciousness. What one has been identifying as "self" actually belongs to parents, grandparents, caretakers. One acts, thinks, feels in particular ways because they did. While many psychotherapies take this direction, they never venture beyond ego. Integral Yoga, on the other hand, foresees a *change of character*—realizing *soul* alone as one's true identity. Many other systems of yoga believe that the character one was born with cannot be changed. The Mother counters these views.

> ... there is something very difficult to do to change your character, because it is not your character which must be changed; it is the character of your antecedents. In them you will not change it (because they have no such intention) but it is in you it must be changed. (Mother, 1972-1987, 4:262)

Dis-identifying with the personality and *identifying* with the psychic being is *the challenging work of yoga*. I can free myself from my antecedents *only* by becoming my authentic self. This notion returns us to Sri Aurobindo's powerful declaration: "Yoga is nothing but practical psychology." (Sri Aurobindo, 1992, p. 39) Though the term *yoga* incorporates breathing practices, postures and dietary or behavioral restrictions, Sri Aurobindo's and Mother's yoga is *primarily inner psychological work which leads to the change and transformation of consciousness*. Yoga is self-analysis: It is making what is unconscious conscious.

> ... if you enter this subconscient, if you let your consciousness infiltrate it, and look carefully, gradually you will discover all the sources, all the origins of all your difficulties; then you will begin to understand what your fathers and mothers, grandfathers and grandmothers were... "I am like that because they were like that." (Mother, 1972-1987, 4:261)

Blurred by ancestral patterns and family conditioning, the self comes into focus through the *psychology of self-perfection*.

> ... we mean by this term [Yoga] a methodised effort towards self-perfection by the expression of the potentialities latent in the being and a union of the human individual with the universal and transcendent Existence we see partially expressed in man and in the Cosmos. (Sri Aurobindo, 1992, p. 2)

Self-exploration and *self-discovery* are germane to the integrated psychotherapies (Mindell, Grof, Raheem). All utilize body, mind, emotions and spirit in a journey recognizing the multiple levels of consciousness of psyche. *Self* refers to a center beyond ego. There is common recognition that psychological death and rebirth are prerequisites for entering the transpersonal realms. Biographically oriented self-exploration and transpersonal realizations are interconnected.

> A gradual working through of the traumatic aspects of one's early history tends to open the way to the perinatal and transpersonal experiences that mediate the spiritual opening. Conversely, individuals who have deep spiritual experiences early in the process of self-exploration ... find subsequent work on the remaining biographical issues much easier and faster. (Grof, 1985, p. 369)

There is a direct connection between traumatic and transpersonal openings. Therapeutically entering her trauma, a woman who had suffered long-term sexual, physical and ritual abuse by her entire family, discovered the presence of the Divine Mother. Grof, Mindell and Raheem concur that "spirituality is an intrinsic property of the psyche that emerges quite spontaneously when the process of self-exploration reaches sufficient depth." (Grof, 1985, p. 368) When the integrated psychotherapies encounter the yoga psychology of Sri Aurobindo and the Mother, the way to the Self by becoming conscious of hidden obstacles is furthered. But permanent realization of the soul as a *replacement* of the ego, followed by subsequent transformation of mind, vital and the physical body, is the distinct objective of yoga psychology.

Psychotherapy is still *crisis driven*—we work on ourselves when we are faced with trauma, loss, illness. Yoga, however, is an *everyday* practice. C. G. Jung recognized the need for ongoing care of psyche. He created *active imagination*, a practice of working with one's inner imagery from night dreams, fantasy and daydreams. This allows a continued dialogue between the ego and the unconscious, ultimately facilitating individuation. Mindell also encourages a similar practice of *inner work* in which one becomes aware of one's *process*—dreams, body symptoms, fantasies. He envisions the body perpetually dreaming: We are called to become *fully aware* of this unfolding of consciousness. These creations of Jung and Mindell come closest to yoga psychology.

While Sri Aurobindo and the Mother advocate a similar process of *inner work*, their emphasis is on soul as the center of individual consciousness. Their yoga encourages ego to move from the center towards the periphery of consciousness, thus initiating *the process of individuation* which allows the ego to retire and the psychic being to reign.

Knowing one's Self in the midst of ever shifting identifications we call "self" can be extremely confusing. In working on the process of self-analysis the Mother advises:

> If this reviewing is to make you progress, you must find something within you in whose light you can be yourself, your own judge, something which represents for you the best part of yourself, which has some light ... and which precisely is in love with progress. Place that before you and first, pass across it as in a cinema all you have done, all that you have felt, your impulses, your thoughts, ... then try to coordinate them ... find out why this has followed that. And look at the luminous screen that is before you: certain things pass by well, without throwing a shadow; others ... throw a little shadow; others ... cast a shadow altogether black and disagreeable. You must do this very sincerely.... (Mother, 1972-1987, 4: 38-40)

Reasoning and morality are not the criteria of such review. Instead, it is the juxtaposition of light and dark that simply exposes unconsciousness and egoism:

> Then you place this egoism before your "light" and ask yourself: "Why has it the right to make me act like that, think like that?"...

you will find in a corner of your being something which thinks and says, "Ah, no, I shall accept everything but that." You will see that it is a petty vanity, a movement of self-love.... (Mother, 1972-1987, 4: 38-40)

This detailed self-inquiry comprises the spade-work of yoga, preparing the ground of the being for transformation. It is equally as important as the exciting influxes of soul, and the higher levels of consciousness. It is a way of "composting" the garbage of the ego.

You will see that the elements which do not conform to your ideal are not generally elements which you have to throw wholly out of yourself ... they are simply things not in their place. If you organize everything—your feelings, your thoughts, your impulses,—around your psychic centre which is the inner light, you will see that all inner disorder will change into a luminous order. (Mother, 1972-1987, 4:40)

Review of our multiple parts eventually reveals the existence of our multiple personalities. Some express the physical ego, others the vital and mental ego. All are in conflict, vying for the role of "top-dog." By witnessing the personality's drama, the light of our psychic being opens the way to our *true individuality*.

Ego is too frail, too unstable, to support the spiritual force of the psyche. For that the psychic being, the soul in the physical body, must come fully into consciousness as the authentic center of the human being. Transfer of knowledge and power to the dwelling place of the immanent Divine within us is the next step of an evolutionary psychology.

4

Bridging Spiritual Practice and Psychotherapy

> True sanity entails in one way or another the dissolution of the normal ego, that false self competently adjusted to our alienated social reality: the emergence of the "inner" archetypal mediators of divine power, and through this death a rebirth, and the eventual reestablishment of a new kind of ego functioning, the ego now being the servant of the Divine, no longer its betrayer. (R.D. Laing, M.D., 1965, p. 60)

IN SHARP CONTRAST TO WESTERN PSYCHIATRY, R.D. Laing's visionary perspective reflects Sri Aurobindo's mapping of the journey from ego to soul. Pioneers of an evolving consciousness, they both recognize that spiritual experience is intrinsic to our psyche and can be accelerated through spiritual practice, psychotherapy or *even* through psychosis. Laing, whose psychiatric work focused on schizophrenia, identified the plight of humanity with its preoccupation with control of the *external world*, thus eclipsing the *inner world*—"the realities of imagination, dreams, fantasies, trances, the realities of contemplative and meditative states...." (Laing, p. 58)

When ego, instrument for surviving in the external world, is fractured or destroyed, the person is suddenly exposed to the inner world. Modern psychiatry categorizes the experiences of this inner world as *pathological*, thus fatally ignoring the *transcendental experience* of both the mystic and the madman.

Laing envisions the task of the psychiatrist/therapist "... to educt the person from this world [external] and induct him to the other [inner]. To guide him in it, and to lead him back again." (Laing, p. 57) Like Ken Wilber, he challenges the traditional role of therapist, envisioning a guide bearing resemblance to a shaman—one who possesses experiential knowledge of the inner terrain and the power to traverse it.

Although Laing's focus is on "psychotic" episodes, a transit may also occur through spiritual practice or psychotherapy. "When a person goes mad, a profound transposition of his position in relation to all domains of being occurs. His center of experience moves from ego to Self." (Laing, p. 53) This movement, however, is a *process* in which ego and Self, natural and supernatural, are often muddled. Whether we label the event "psychosis," "spiritual practice" or "psychotherapy," *crisis* is present—*death* and *rebirth* are the common feature. In the passage from the outer personality to the inner being, Sri Aurobindo describes an *intermediate zone* where the traveler is confused by conflicting claims of the inner and outer worlds. Experiences in this realm of psyche bear a strong resemblance to "psychosis."

> This intermediate zone is a region of half-truths—.... The sadhak [practitioner] thinks that he is no longer in the old small consciousness at all, because he feels in contact with something larger or more powerful, and yet the old consciousness is still there, not really abolished. He feels the control or influence of some Power, Being or Force greater than himself, aspires to be its instrument and thinks he has got rid of ego; but this delusion of egolessness often covers an exaggerated ego. (Sri Aurobindo, 1995, p. 1042)

Both the person believing that he is Jesus Christ and the spiritual aspirant may wander for a long time in this treacherous zone of consciousness; some never emerge.

The triggers for initiation into this passage are numerous. Entry into inner worlds may even occur spontaneously. Our main focus in this chapter is on the use of skillful means to bridge psychotherapy and spiritual practice.

Spontaneous Openings

Extreme mental, emotional and physical phenomena that disrupt normal ego functioning and cause crises are playing a role in the evolution of consciousness. These altered states of consciousness—like visions of goddesses and demons, extreme heat in the spine accompanied by uncontrollable bodily movements, awareness of spiritual guides or inhabitants of the underworld, oneness with the entire universe and near-death experiences— can be evoked by intense spiritual practice, psychedelics or by the psychotherapeutic process. Others occur spontaneously without invitation demonstrating that the evolutionary pressure of consciousness overrides all personal wishes.

Bob, a jazz musician in his mid-sixties, consulted me about a singular change in his consciousness. Recently retired from a teaching career, he looked forward to playing music and tennis when, during a period of intense piano practice, the change occurred. He began to suffer physical symptoms of extreme pressure and heat in his head, symptoms relieved only by staring into space and focusing his eyes towards the crown of his head. Eventually, he identified with a single point in a vast energy field, a point of profound peace and awareness. His personality had become inconsequential.

Eventually, however, he became terrified: Would he be able to return from that vast energy field? This fear, a fear of losing his mind, existed in tandem with his difficulty in reestablishing a relationship with the ordinary world. A seasoned musician, he was losing his ability to perform. Lapses also occurred on the tennis court in the midst of returning a ball.

Beckoned by the "other consciousness," his capacity for intimate relationship became severely limited, presenting a major challenge to his life partner. Was there an "organic" explanation for this bizarre phenomenon? Should he take medication?

My approach to working with Bob was process-oriented. I consistently supported each experience, whether based on fear or an emerging "other consciousness." His process did not demand the normal psychotherapeutic effort to uncover and amplify feelings, images, bodily symptoms. It demanded coping strategies, as well as creative ways to ground this new and overwhelming energy.

Bob underwent standard neurological tests, receiving a clean bill of physical health. I did not recognize any mental or emotional pathology. What I did recognize were *very* strong signals of kundalini energy—extreme heat, pressure in the head, inner sounds of cicadas, eyes rolling upward and converging on a point above the crown center (single-sight). Above all, Bob's entry into the "other consciousness" endowed him with both a greater awareness and a deeper sense of peace. He was able to witness in great minute detail the various parts of his personality—though illuminating, this process also evoked emotional pain and depression.

As I followed his process, I introduced Bob to the writings of Sri Aurobindo and Ken Wilber. Receiving immense clarity from these "giants," he has begun to explore his spirituality. Resonance with the experiences of others has slowly softened negative judgment of his own experience; he no longer thinks of it as an aberration.

Bob's greatest challenge was to build a bridge between two worlds of radically different consciousness. He discovered that in avoiding his inner world, he inflicted upon himself both physical and psychological pain. Gradually, regularly, he began to "sit and stare"—his own creative form of meditation. Physical work, tennis and bodywork helped him to stay in his body and relate to the ordinary world.

Bob's journey is a work in progress. For six years, he has experienced a steadily increasing consciousness. This has significantly accelerated his personal psychological work, while simultaneously affording him direct access to his spiritual reality. His experience is a testimony to the evolutionary pressure of consciousness—a consciousness which transcends all personal designs and efforts. (See Chapter 8, An Uninvited Guest)

The Spiritual Door

Passage from the ego to the inner being can be opened through the discipline of either spiritual practice or psychotherapy. Although these disciplines have differing goals, some of their methods overlap and can be mutually beneficial. However, both practices possess an inability and a resistance to work with emerging "psychological" and "spiritual" material. Intensive meditation can produce psychosis; psychotherapy can release kundalini. In either case a *helper* or *guide* is important. In the spiritual context, a teacher is necessary. In a psychological framework, the therapist takes on a new role—that of an *integral guide*. This guide must undergo extensive training in psychotherapy *and* spiritual practice in order to bridge the personal and transpersonal. The *integral guide* must possess a knowledge of the body, mind, life-force and spiritual realms in order to follow and support the traveler's process in both outer and inner worlds. In order to expedite a particular journey s/he may collaborate with other guides possessing such specialized training as shamanism.

The journey inward is unique to each traveler. For the spiritual practitioner, it may begin by following the breath, or by visualization in order to focus and eventually quiet the mind. Initially, one might experience a state of harmony and peace. However, this state is only the beginning of a long and sometimes

perilous passage. Jack Kornfield, a teacher of Buddhist meditation, discriminates between *two levels of spiritual practice*:

> One begins with virtue and concentration and calming and a
> softening of the body and an opening of the heart... But then
> when we are ready to go deeper, it means to open the whole of
> the inner world. What this requires of us is a willingness to face
> pleasure and pain equally, to open, to touch ... "the whole
> catastrophe" and to look directly into the light and the shadow
> of the heart and mind. (Kornfield, 1989, p. 154)

To open the whole of the inner world is reminiscent of the
Mother's charge that "you must take apart the entire machinery
of your being." During this process it is not uncommon for even
seasoned practitioners to find themselves in *crisis* or *spiritual
emergency*.

A monk who had completed many meditation retreats entered into therapy with me. While meditating he encountered a
black depression. He began using alcohol as an escape and was
eventually asked to leave the monastery. Treatment involved
psychotherapy in order to deal with unresolved family issues,
addiction and depression. Neither the monastery nor his spiritual
practice had been able to remove these emotional and psychological obstacles.

While spiritual and psychotherapeutic processes are both
"inner practices," there are often mistaken *attitudes* about
therapy in spiritual communities. The monk who was forced to
leave his monastery felt he had failed in his spiritual practice.
Since he believed the spiritual dimension was higher than the
psychological, spiritual experience should have been sufficient to
transform all the other levels of his being:

Kornfield reminds us:

> In this process there are no higher or lower levels, no areas that
> are more sacred than any other. There is simply the encounter-

ing of whatever patterns of contraction, fear and identification cause our suffering and discovering an awakening and freedom from them. (Kornfield, 1993, p. 246)

As in the case of the monk, the length and intensity of our spiritual practice does not necessarily free us of personal and developmental obstacles to liberation. Trauma can generate such fear and dread that the practitioner may unconsciously *use* spiritual practice to avoid facing the truth. When the trauma is not addressed, we find ourselves arrested in our spiritual growth.

Fortunately, there are today a growing number of therapists possessing integral training who are as adept in working with a spiritual as well as a traumatic process. In this awesome work of exploring our inner world, of examining the entire machinery of our being, we need the combined wisdom and power of psychology *and* spirituality.

The Psychotherapeutic Door

1. The Inner Healer

The sacred space of psychotherapy is often the catalyst that transports us to transpersonal or spiritual realms. An untapped psychic force may enter our personal drama as *ally* helping us to resolve a seemingly intractable issue.

Rachel, in her mid-fifties and pursuing a strong Buddhist practice, had periodically been in therapy with me for about ten years. As a young mother, she had lost contact with her two children. Years later, at age sixteen, her son suffered a psychotic breakdown. She worked hard in both therapy and in her spiritual practice to cleanse herself from guilt and anguish. Although she was successful in alleviating much of her agony, the shadow of this deep wounding remained. From time to time it would rise again, and she would return to work with me.

For years an inner feminine figure appeared to Rachel—
sometimes in meditation, sometimes spontaneously. She called
her "the woman in the desert, Red Dirt woman, the crone."

> ...that elusive figure that first appeared to the right of my head,
> sitting still, facing the mountains. Only her dark, clay cloak was
> visible. She seemed forbidding, alternately fierce and elusive.
> Our relationship was visceral, graphic. Few words; images of
> eagle talons ripping off the top of my head, dark tunnels, cliffs,
> squatting in primal muck, blood, bones, screeches—all in im-
> penetrable silence.
>
> When I went out West, I thought her presence would be
> stronger, but no ... I came back saying that I had killed her; she
> was only in my mind and I didn't need her anymore. I think I
> was angry and saw her as withholding. Her message often
> seemed foreboding, taunting, as if I wasn't really ready to come
> as close as I thought I wanted to be. She was a Don Juan force
> to me. Before her "death" I had a lovely vision of myself
> standing by her. I was almost pure energy. There was such
> purity, love, emptiness, but then it was gone. (Private commu-
> nication)

Upon resuming therapy with me, I suggested she invite this
powerful ally into her therapeutic work again. During body-
centered work (process acupressure), she opened to an autonomous energy, moving her body into bizarre positions: Spontaneously arching, the top of her head rested on the table; her arms
pulled back, while her elbows met at her spine; her hands, claw-
like, poised above her body; her legs pulled up, feet touching; and
her face contorted. There was no verbal exchange during these
sessions, but she told me later that she felt very "bird-like." As for
the inner woman, she was no longer in visual form.

> I found she was no longer to the right, but behind me. She has
> always been without form except for the cloak or serape, but

now I found myself *backing* into her energy. At first I felt
embraced by her, yet lonely since she was no longer visible—just
a cloak around me. I began to draw on her again, and take
comfort in her presence as a true inner self. (Private communication)

During our work with this inner teacher, Rachel decided to
contact her alone. After some breathing and deep relaxation she
received two Spanish words, *alma*—soul or spirit, and *corazon*—
heart or core. A great peace and joy descended as she received the
following vision:

The woman was lying on her right side in a fetal pose against
some big yellow boulders. My body arched and I realized she
was lying against my heart (the boulders). We had an exchange
about my needing to open my heart—break it up, be kinder and
more compassionate. I asked for her help. She rose and with a
sword of white light struck again and again, shattering the
boulders. I felt such gratitude and love, I wept. Then she sat
down and began to eat the pieces of my heart. As she sat there
with blood running down the sides of her mouth, she asked me
to join her. Feeling the pieces enter my stomach, I thought that
my heart was now everywhere in my body. (Private communication)

In this work, *alma corazon* is the true healer—a healer who
probed beyond Rachel's psychological wounding into her spiritual depths. Although this journey is distinctly *shamanic*, the
teaching transmitted is Buddhist. It is a visceral teaching on
emptiness and *groundlessness*. Alma, barely with form, eventually
disappears, becoming the energy which moves Rachel to shape-
shift from human to bird. She is teaching her that *all form* is
insubstantial, ultimately *empty*—even the form of her suffering
son, the form of Alma, the form of herself; and, finally, *the form
of the very teaching itself* (a teaching that *opens a heart* contracted

by suffering). As she wields the sword of white light, Alma challenges Rachel to die, to be reborn with her heart omnipresent.

Rachel's passage represents a powerful convergence of psychological and spiritual perception. Alma, an *inner archetypal mediator of divine power,* emerges from the depths of psyche to confront the ego-formation constellated by her relationship with her son. She asks for nothing less than *surrender*—to open to *bodhichitta*, where mind and heart are one. In this work, I acted as midwife, minimally facilitating the birth process.

2. Stories of Trauma and Transcendence

The release of traumatic memories into consciousness often offers entry into the spiritual realm. Living in a world beset by war and violence, all of us suffer subliminal terror. Those coming for therapy have generally been wounded by personal trauma. Paradoxically, unraveling their trauma may create an opening into a higher state of consciousness.

The construction of a survival self during and after invasion by an overwhelming force serves many purposes: (1) Immediate survival of the trauma itself; (2) keeping those powerful forces at bay until the survivor gains sufficient strength to deal with them; (3) guarding of the victim against further attacks from both the world and the psyche.

Trauma prematurely tears the veil between our personal consciousness and the transpersonal forces of our inner world. Confrontation between these two worlds creates a crisis not only at the inception of the traumatic event, but in its re-accessing. The guide in this transit must possess the tools and the deep knowledge of the traveler's inner and outer terrain. A trusting relationship between guide and traveler must ensue if the latter's inner world is to reveal not only the hidden trauma, but also those transpersonal guides who offer clarity and protection in the reconstitution of a new self. Finally, the traveler must *integrate* the experiences of the inner journey and learn to relate from a new center.

Transpersonal healing forces abound in trauma work. They manifest in the struggle between life and death to protect and give succor, and guide the victim across the abyss of fear. Not only are they present in the original assault, they appear again when the unhealed wound is touched. While trauma often blocks spiritual opening, *it can also directly access it.*

Maura, in her mid-fifties, entered psychotherapy while leaving an abusive marriage. Her life-long pattern of flight stemmed from the physical and sexual abuse inflicted by her family of origin. After graduating high school, she joined a religious order, but discovered that it was neither a panacea nor a cure for her fear and her alcoholism.

After weeks of confronting her abuse in therapy, she began to tremble and cry, "They are always watching me! If I say anything they will kill me!" Initially, this utterance made no sense to either of us; however, after beginning process acupressure, Maura was flooded with early memories. She and her infant sister had been buried alive in a ritual of torture and abuse, Maura being placed in the grave on her back, while her sister lay on top of her, face down.

She wept and groaned as traumatic remembrances shocked her body violently. Sessions of this nature continued for more than a month. One day, she sat quietly crying for a half-hour as if her heart would break. Had another childhood demon surfaced?' Gradually, however, the crying subsided and Maura declared, "My tears are tears of gratitude," she said incredulously, "My soul has entered my body, at last."

While this realization did not mark the end of this torturous passage, it infused Maura with new strength and direction. She ended the abusive relationship with her husband, established a new career and continued the work of freeing her Self. Her childhood's simulated burial had been responsible for her soul's departure. Was her *conscious* near-death experience now responsible for its return?

*   *   *   *

Trauma victimizes with an annihilating force that closes down—to varying degrees—the normal parameters of mind, emotions and body. Survival depends on a number of possible strategies: (1) Trauma victims might dissociate from their primary personality by adopting one or more alternate personalities existing in the psyche. They might abandon their physical body, by entering the subtle energy body. During automobile accidents and operations, for example, people often view their physical body from above. Or, they might take temporary refuge in the inner being's subtle energy form.

Lisa, a woman who took refuge in the subtle being, had been tortured and brainwashed from an early age. She survived by entering the energy centers (chakras) of her body. In an initial meeting, she identified herself as a "survivor of sexual abuse." However, unearthing her trauma revealed deeper abuse, accompanied by extraordinary survival skills. Process acupressure led her to three past lives: A young boy separated from his parents, a Confederate soldier suffering from a head wound, and an Indian woman faced with the choice of staying in her village or exploring the larger world.

Lisa fully assumed the personality in each story. She regressed to the small boy, terrified and sobbing for his lost parents. As a Confederate soldier, she spoke in a strong Southern drawl, expressing the suffering he endured from his injuries. As I observed the emergence of these divergent personalities, I marveled at the force that had opened her inner being.

After three sessions, Lisa entered the trauma of her *present* life in which she suddenly received a clear image of her own father urinating and masturbating on her as a small child. Startled, she abruptly came out of trance. The devastating image opened the way to an extremely dark passage—a passage that threatened to annihilate her.

During process acupressure she regressed to childhood where she suffered psychological conditioning as she was being sexually abused. Though she knew several people were present, she only recognized her father. Whispering in her tiny child's voice, Lisa alerted me, "They are trying to take my soul. If I make myself very small, I can go into the yellow color near my navel. My soul is hidden inside."

Saying that they were "operating" on her, the group had sex with Lisa. Simultaneously, they called her the "bride of the devil" and taught her to say prayers backwards. They also showed her an image of Jesus hanging upside down on the cross. During this abuse she had to chant, "Black is red, red is black," and was forced to eat raw liver. While consuming the meat, she was taught to repeat, "De-*liver* us *to* evil."

Overwhelmingly confused and sexually abused, Lisa became aware of energy centers in which she could take refuge. Becoming very still, she whispered, "I am inside now ... in the energy. The fairies told me to go to the bottom of the ocean so I can get clean." The way out of this horrific world was to go inward—towards the subliminal realm of her soul. Here she discovered a temporary asylum where she could protect her sanity and her core identity.

*   *   *   *

Paul, a coordinator in the film industry, came to therapy to work on relationship and intimacy issues. He knew that he had been sexually abused by both parents and brutally beaten by his father. Although he experienced *mental* flashbacks of this abuse, he doubted their veracity, dissociating from them.

Paul had two brothers and a sister. His sister remembered being sexually abused by their father; his brothers recalled their father's violence. Paul had hazy memories of an elder brother, Alexander, his friend and protector. One day he recalled a hideous, bloody scene in which his father kicked Alexander in the head. Whenever Paul asked either of his parents about Alexander's death, he was told that his brother died of a tumor. No family photos of Alexander existed. There was no funeral for him.

Another devastating memory revealed to Paul that he could have suffered the same fate as his older brother. The mother used Paul for sexual gratification. When Paul's father discovered mother and son together his rage exploded. Breaking Paul's nose, he locked him in a closet. Faintly, Paul overheard his mother pleading with her husband not to kill their son.

Initially, I attempted to unlock Paul's sensory and emotional being through process acupressure but physical contact was too overwhelming for him. However, holotropic breathwork helped him to release body armor and access bodily, emotional and mental memories. In the wake of his devastating past and the terror he experienced in its recollection, Paul called upon his own spiritual guidance. Asking for help during this process, we meditated together. In session, he returned to his childhood prison— the closet. He received a clear message, "During your childhood we were present to guide and protect you. We are here now for the same purpose." Their communication imparted to him an inconceivable strength and courage.

Within minutes of beginning each breathwork session, Paul palpably encountered the traumatic events of his childhood: oral sex with his mother; rape and beatings by his father; the brutal killing of his brother. He entered each event either as observer or participant, perceiving every image with unprecedented clarity. The power of breath had transported him to his hidden story.

Accessing emotional and physical sensibilities that had been previously unavailable, the door to Paul's past opened. Courageously, he withstood the memory of a violent attack in which his father wielded a baseball bat on him. In an attempt to protect Paul, his older brother, Alexander, lost his life. In another perversely violent assault, Paul remembered his father suffocating him as he raped him. In our session, Paul re-experienced the intensity of suffocation and rape: "I watched myself die—floating, falling into a black hole, separating from my body, but something stopped my fall and a voice said, 'It's not time yet. Let's go back.'"

When Paul entered therapy, he had only fleeting mental recollections. But revelation and self-acceptance became possible for him when his body remembered the aberrations it had withstood and the transpersonal guidance it had received. This guidance provided support and the possibility of renewal. It provided a ground when all ordinary ground had disappeared.

*   *   *   *

The path of trauma does not always lead to the world of spirit. Sometimes it leads to breakdown. Broken emotionally, physically and mentally, one can remain trapped in corridors without exit. Sometimes, irreparably wounded, the victim's life becomes severely limited—medicated, isolated, devoid of intimacy.

However, I am also encountering in ever growing numbers those victims of abuse who discover transpersonal, healing agents within the healing event. These discoveries transform trauma from ongoing disaster to new growth. Healing trauma requires a force that goes beyond duality—a spiritual force. Healers trained to recognize the presence of spiritual forces in the traumatic experience can re-direct victims from drifting down paths without exit to discovering doors that open to the spirit.

*   *   *   *

Julia suffered assaults so overpowering, they could have driven her to insanity or suicide. Several potent factors contributed to her survival—her capacity to do battle with the energies of her torturers; her strength of body and mind; and her discovery of sanctuaries within and beyond her body. (See Part II, Chapter 3.) The relationship between trauma and transcendence in her story is noteworthy here.

Julia was already conscious of early sexual abuse by her sister, and brutal beatings by her father, when she came to work with me. Although *mentally* aware of these events, she had never fully acknowledged to herself their traumatic impact. Process acupressure immediately opened her body; shaking violently, she began to remember the horrific abuse. This process eventually revealed her entire story—a story far darker than her initial memories.

The underworld of Julia's psyche uncovered a network of familial aberrations. Her sister's sexual abuse from ages seven to nine appeared first, followed by her father's brutality from ages three to twelve and rape by her father throughout her teenage years. A darker underpinning ultimately emerged—*ritual abuse*. At age four, Julia was forced into rituals conducted by her mother and maternal uncle. She remembered lying naked on a slab of marble while her mother cut her under the right shoulder blade, drawing blood. She was also forced to witness the sacrifice of animals.

Julia's bodily memories opened the way to awareness of repressed traumatic experiences. For a body that had been so violated, it was amazingly conscious. From a very young age she had been trained in gymnastics, competitive swimming and dance. Also educated as a body worker, she possessed the sensitive gift of *knowing others through the body*—a gift developed, no doubt, from the torture she herself had suffered.

Julia's dark passage repeatedly exposed her to death. Death of the physical body. Loss of the soul. These multiple near-death experiences trained her in the art of exiting and re-entering her body. When under violent attack by her father, she entered other bodies—even her father's, as well as designs and colors. Often she needed to go far away—into a galaxy or into white light.

The impact sent me hurtling from my body,
Racing, as if electrocuted, through the pathways of my spine,
Shooting explosively and excruciatingly out the top of my head
Into a blinding white light. (*Wrenching*, unpublished poem)

Julia's spine became so sensitized, so charged with electrical energy, that she often wondered if her torture included *electrical shock*. This great charge of electricity was activated, I believe, by her need to escape her body through her spine. Her many escape routes—galaxies, other bodies, white light—also included time travel.

Out of my head I rushed,
Traveling backwards through thousands of years,
I was like a fish or snake who is only spine,
Moved by a single undulating force through a liquid atmosphere, limbless. (*Green*, unpublished poem)

Eventually, Julia's explorations led her to the goddess, the Divine Feminine principle. Throughout our work, she longed for her feminine side—a side she was forced to hide from her abusers. The family myth of Julia cast her as the strongest arm wrestler, swimmer and gymnast. Ironically, this arch-competitor was the sacrificial offering in her mother's and uncle's strange rituals.

As we unveiled the many worlds of Julia's abuse, she met the Goddess several times. Experiencing this light-filled, beautiful woman, she realized that divine intervention had come when she could no longer leave her body through the escape route of her spine.

During her teenage years when her father was raping her, pain and chaos had become unbearable:

I would not have made it without Her,
She who arrived to carry me away,

Effortlessly removing me from my shocked and shattered body,
And revealing to me the Other Place
Where the air was a light stroke upon my skin,
And colors of cool melon and warm embers combined.
(*Wrenching*, unpublished poem)

Her relationship with the Goddess grew steadily. Re-experiencing excruciating moments of torture, Julia was transported into the transpersonal realms. The gentle, powerful Goddess had become a central figure in her reclamation.

*   *   *   *

The Role of the Therapist in Integral Practice

The stories presented in this chapter, and throughout this book, are signposts pointing to an evolutionary leap in the field of psychology. Many psychotherapeutic and spiritual practitioners are no longer content to circle around the tether post of ego. They aspire to a deeper consciousness—*a new center*—while honoring the boundaries and goals of their particular practice.

A psychology addressing only the surface personality and the building of a strong ego will not further true healing: The movement from an ego-centered to a soul-centered psychology demands an *integral vision* of the human being as well as the means to unite the disparate dimensions of mind, life-force, body and spirit. Realistically, however, incorporation of the transpersonal into psychotherapy will necessitate a major philosophical re-orientation as well as a fundamental paradigm shift. Presently, when transpersonal material emerges in psychotherapy:

> Many of the experiences that occur ... are so extraordinary and seemingly absurd that an average therapist feels uncomfortable with them, finds it difficult to see how they could be of any therapeutic value, and tends to discourage them explicitly or implicitly. There is a strong tendency among professionals to

interpret transpersonal phenomena as manifestations of bio-
graphical material in symbolic disguise, as expressions of resistance against painful traumatic memories, as experiential oddi-
ties without any deeper significance, or even as indications of a
psychotic area that the client should stay away from. (Grof,
1985, pp. 376-7)

In working within the framework of Sri Aurobindo's paradigm of the human psyche I have discovered a field large enough
to accommodate both traumatic memories *and* the spiritual
dimension. However, as Grof indicates, the therapist, depending
on his conceptual framework, may shipwreck the very healing
process he is attempting to mid-wife. We must *grow into this new
paradigm* by witnessing our narrow "reality filters" and adopting
a curious *beginner's mind* while dropping our assumption regarding the nature of reality as well as our favorite psychological
theories.

*   *   *   *

We have seen that supporting and following the integral
process gives us access to deep reservoirs of healing. Often the
images opening the way to these transformations cannot be
understood with the rational mind; frequently, they are preceded
by a death-rebirth experience wherein the explorer is faced with
his deepest fear.

Possessed by deep fear for his entire life, Robert suffered
from social isolation in his private life and intellectual isolation in
a job that fell far below his ability. Though possessing a profound
psychic-intuitive capacity, fear blocked access to this deeper
knowledge.

During holotropic breathwork he had this experience:

I thought nothing was going to happen and then I saw the
Other Side in gray that gradually grew brighter. Falling back

into my body, I focused on breathing even more rapidly. Suddenly, I felt the fear spreading from my navel into my entire chest. I believed death was imminent; however, after a struggle I entered the orange honeycomb.

I was in Nirvana.

Eventually, the honeycomb expanded into a bright orange dome and a profound peace permeated my whole being. (Private communication)

Subsequently, Robert realized that he could enter the Other Side by using his psychic-intuitive gift. "My body has always feared that it would die *if I use this gift*. However, since touching the realm of the orange honeycomb, I know I will not die."

Journeying from outer ego consciousness to the vastness of our inner being, we meet the Guardians of the threshold between these realms—the most powerful Guardian is the fear of death. Whether this fear arises from abuse, or an inner Reality, exploring and harnessing the most potent discoveries of contemporary psychology and spirituality for this conquest is the frontier of an evolutionary psychology.

PART II

THE PROCESS OF
INTEGRAL PSYCHOLOGY

The following four stories illustrate the practice of gaining awareness of the full spectrum of consciousness in the healing process. In these stories, birth, death, spiritual emergency, transforming trauma and contact with the transpersonal have become vehicles of conscious evolution that cross traditional and developmental boundaries. Each story reveals a personal process which unfolds in a new awareness of creative possibilities—an awareness accessible to all human beings.

These tales of transformation invite the reader into four unique worlds that unveil the interplay between personal and transpersonal realities. In lives that are distinctly different yet remarkably comparable, each individual has experienced a growth of consciousness from contact with personal and transpersonal dimensions. By accessing this integral wholeness each person in his or her own way has transformed an obstacle, explored a higher aspiration and furthered the journey towards liberation.

May their stories inspire and serve others on the same road.

5

The Suffocated Soul

9:15 PM, AUGUST 12, 2000. The phone rings. I know instantly that it is the call I have been expecting for three days. I hear Steven's voice, "Carrie just left her body. I am holding her, and I *know* she hears us." Feelings of relief and loss sweep through me. Relief, because the suffering is over, her incredible journey is complete. Loss, because of the pain of separation: In pursuit of her soul, Carrie and I had achieved a rare intimacy.

Five years before, a clinical psychologist called me, requesting that I work with Carrie, "She has lung cancer. I don't know how to help." Within a few days Carrie walked into my office.

Coiffed in a brightly colored scarf, a small, intense woman in her mid-thirties entered my office. Her eyes conveyed fear and apprehension, but her presence conveyed courage. Seating herself quickly, she welcomed me into her world of pain and fear. Our first task was to clear any debris from the relationship with her previous therapist. Diagnosed with lung cancer, Carrie had had two operations on her right lung. In the second operation doctors removed the lung, but discovered cancer in the remaining one. They pronounced her terminally ill—stage four cancer. She was devastated. Why must she die at such a young age? How could she face separation from her two-year-old daughter? Long repressed emotions poured forth. She decided to see a therapist. Both therapist and husband, relayed the same message: "Think positively. Don't cry." This was a message she had heard since childhood: The family's emotional taboo had surfaced again. After her diagnosis, Carrie, her mother and sister, were all crying when her father entered the room. "Stop!" he commanded.

Resurrecting long-buried emotions were to become a major part of my work with Carrie.

On July 7, 1994, Carrie heard her death knell, "You have cancer." In her first surgery, doctors removed the middle lobe of her right lung. Though she was told that the surgery was successful, Carrie lived in fear and agonizing pain for months. During this period she visited the psychotherapist who told her to think positively.

Three months after surgery the cancer reappeared on the CT scans. The doctors decided that the rest of the right lung had to be removed, followed by four to six cycles of chemotherapy. This diagnosis generated suicidal feelings in Carrie, but because of her two-year-old daughter, and her strong will to live, she consented. Subsequent to the surgery, most of the lung was found to be healthy, but several cancerous spots persisted.

After only three cycles of chemotherapy, CT scans were advised again. The cancer now appeared in her left lung—stage four, incurable and terminal: Her expected life span was six months. Still, Carrie did not give up. "Okay," she said to herself, "I am going to die. Now I need to learn how to live." It was during chemotherapy that Carrie's search for alternative therapies began. After nine months, she refused chemotherapy. One and a half years after being diagnosed, she refused all conventional medicine.

Carrie entered my life with her dreams. Never had she paid attention to her dream life: She had no spiritual orientation. Scientific, with a Ph.D. in biology, ideas of soul, inner being or the significance of dreams, were strange to her. The first dream, experienced one month after diagnosis of incurable cancer, served as a blueprint for our ensuing exploration. "About 1 A.M.

I was awakened by a powerful dream. I arose, confused about what was reality and what was dream."

Here is the dream:

I am home waiting for someone I call an "adviser." I am sitting at the kitchen table talking to a friend. I tell this person that Steven (husband) and I are going to take a trip around the world. I don't know where we are going, but we will make a lot of stops.

The adviser comes to my front door. I intend to tell him about my recurrent dream, but first I must wait for a young woman who was there before me. When it is my turn, I tell him the dream.

In these recurrent dreams I always have a mouth full of "stuff"—either a gummy substance or wads of paper towels. Although the details of the dream differ slightly, the common theme is about the existence of large amounts of stuff in my mouth, and my struggle to remove it. Even when I managed to remove some, more would immediately accumulate. I couldn't talk and no one in my dreams could hear me. No one noticed my struggle.

I told the adviser that I had dreamt this many times in my life, and could he tell me its meaning. He responded very calmly, "You have to find the Hindu and ask him." Furious at his ambiguous response I cried, "I have no idea what you are talking about!" Sensing that he was giving me critical information, I was frustrated because he wouldn't tell me more.

In the next moment I was in bed thinking I was awakening from the dream. Then I started feeling this stuff in my mouth again. I began to panic, this time because I thought I was awake. I said to myself, "What the hell is going on? This is supposed to be a dream and now it is real life!" I tried to scream but no sound came because of the stuff in my mouth. I felt I was suffocating, struggling and screaming inside myself.

Steven was sitting in bed next to me, but he was looking the other way, out of a large window. He did not hear me or see my struggle. I started to fall out of bed, struggling to scream for help, when the dream ended.

A dream within a dream—in which Carrie was relating a recurrent dream—this could not be deciphered in a few sittings. The center of the dream, for Carrie, was the adviser's message, "You have to find the Hindu and ask him." Awareness of this message marked the turning point of her work with the cancer. It marked the beginning of a healing journey which was to reveal her soul.

We worked on this dream over a period of five years—until just a few days before she left her body. All of the elements of her psychological and spiritual work were present. Some images she recognized immediately. Others, she did not recognize for years. Together, we worked on the mysterious image of the Hindu which Carrie had carried for months. Then, in one of our sessions, it became instantly clear. I asked her,

> "Carrie, what do you know about Hindus?"
> "I don't know anything except that they live in India."
> "Do you have an image of a Hindu?"
> "I'm not sure," Carrie replied, "but I picture him wearing a turban." Suddenly, she put her hands on her head. The cloth wrapped around, to cover her hair loss from chemotherapy, was, in fact, called a turban. Realization flooded her.
> "The Hindu is my Self!" Carrie exclaimed.

This was a profound awakening.
Excited, Carrie continued:

The dream was telling me that the person to ask about my recurrent dream of stuff in my mouth was *myself*! It told me not only to ask the Hindu, but to *find* him. I had to find my inner self! What an incredible revelation this was to me. Until then, I had no idea what it meant to listen to my inner self.

She had taken a quantum leap toward her own transformation! Again and again, she insisted, "I began to live *after* I received my cancer diagnosis: Before, I didn't feel anything." Discovering her inner self exacerbated Carrie's healing process which now included acupuncture/Chinese herbs, journal writing, cancer workshops e.g., Simonton Cancer Counseling Center, nutrition (juicing and vegetarian diet), walking one to two miles daily and reading extensively on cancer, healing, living and dying.

Our transpersonal work continued to evolve.

Accessing the buried emotions of her entire life, we explored her dreams, her guides into the unexplored territory of her Self; process acupressure, visualization, meditation and, in the last months of her life, the direct embracing of her dying process. She began to dialogue with her soul, and wrote instructions on how to be *cared* for spiritually at the time of her passage from her body.

Examining her "big dream," we confronted her fear of the cancer: She did not want to look at it; she simply wanted to get rid of it.

During process acupressure, Carrie accessed vital information about the cancer through her visual channel.

> The cancer in my lung looked like black holes, five of them as indicated by the CT scan. But how do you get rid of holes? I was very distressed by this image; it made me feel helpless.

Upon first seeing the cancer, terrified of meeting the enemy head-on, Carrie cried without stop. Centering on her image of the cancer, I created a relaxation and guided imagery tape. She also went to the Simonton Center, continuing to use creative imagery in dealing with the black holes.

> I saw my immune system as ants that could crawl into the holes and clean them out. Over time, my image changed to ants with large front teeth which fit perfectly into the holes.

It was through her meditation that Carrie eventually discovered the cause of her cancer. "I had *suffocated my soul*," she cried. The dream image of choking on the "stuff" in her mouth was symbolic of the literal threat of suffocation (of impaired lungs) which she endured. Relating this theme of suffocation to her cancer imagery of black holes, she said, "It was as if I had tried to create tunnels to breathe because I was suffocating myself."

Our next layer of work focused on learning why Carrie had suffocated her soul and how to reverse the process. "I had, indeed, emotionally suffocated myself throughout my life," she exclaimed. Following her dream life, using process acupressure to open blocked energy, Carrie embarked on the "heroine's journey."

She would leave no stone unturned in her quest to find her soul.

In this quest Carrie realized that there is a major difference between expressing *thoughts*, and expressing *feelings*. From her father she had learned not to reveal emotional pain—eventually it would go away. From her mother she had learned to cry alone. Battling the family's repression, her older sister was labeled the "problem child." By choosing the "quiet path," Carrie became the favored child.

In her childhood and adolescence, Carrie encountered death twice. A dream revealed the significance of both deaths.

I dreamt I went to a healer to learn how to heal myself from cancer. I gave the healer a large pile of papers which were a compilation of my life story. The healer read my story and said, "You forgot to include the story of the turtle." I looked at her in amazement. How did she know about the turtle? It was not in the papers I gave her. Why was the story of the turtle important?

In writing the story of her pet turtle's death, repressed memories surfaced. At first, Carrie could not even remember going to her grandmother's funeral. Recall at burying her turtle in the rain triggered recall of her grandmother's burial.

Loss of her grandmother was traumatic. Though they were extremely close, no one told Carrie that her grandmother had cancer. She was not allowed to go to her funeral, and no one shared their feelings after her death. Many vital family relationships were severed: After a fight between her father and grandfather, Carrie never saw her grandfather again.

For twenty years, Carrie repressed her grief, fear and sadness. Releasing these feelings in our sessions, she returned to her grandmother's grave site. She wrote her grandmother a letter, and created a ritual in which she relived the death. She even processed events around this death *with both her mother and father*.

Resurrecting this early trauma opened the way for other resurrections. Just before Carrie stopped chemotherapy, the image of an old boyfriend surfaced in a dream. We worked on this buried memory for months. I was awed by the extent of Carrie's persistence.

Before Carrie met her husband Steven, she had had a five-year relationship with a Japanese man. She loved him deeply, but knew when she first met Hiko that the relationship would not last. He was in the United States temporarily, as a student, and would return to Japan when his studies were over. Both Carrie and Hiko were pursuing Ph.D. degrees. As his work ended, the fateful separation drew close. Neither could speak of this separation, "It was like knowing that someone was going to die. I didn't stop loving him because I knew he would leave me. Perhaps, one loves even more."

Six months before Hiko's departure Carrie met her husband-to-be. Once again, she fell in love. However, "I did not love Hiko any less. I loved them both, but had to choose." Carrie told Hiko about Steven. They had a final meeting. "I felt I had to say good-bye quickly—I thought this would reduce the pain. He drove me home. Without a word, I turned from him and ran into my apartment. I never saw Hiko again."

A month later Hiko wrote Carrie a letter expressing gratitude for their relationship. Though she kept the letter, she never responded. She had internalized the behavior of her parents: When confronted with emotional pain, avoid it and it will go away. This method did not work for Carrie. Thoughts of Hiko rose again; he even appeared in her dreams. She had pushed him away, but now, "I knew that if I were to heal, I had to acknowledge the loss—and express the grief."

Carrie decided to write Hiko. For him, she wrote one letter which was informational; for herself, she wrote one which was emotional. She was amazed at her own tears. Hiko answered, and eventually called to say he would be visiting the USA. A few weeks before he came, Carrie had several dreams in which she tried to talk to him. She felt that talking to Hiko would lead toward spiritual growth.

When he arrived in Atlanta, they spoke on the phone for fifteen minutes. Nothing was communicated emotionally; but the unconscious communicated to her in her dream world:

> I found Hiko hanging on a ladder, extremely tired, not looking well. Someone had left him there and he could not get down. I helped him down and he said he must attend a meeting. Watching him go into a room, I closed the door behind him.

We worked on the image of Hiko being left hanging. What had been left hanging in their relationship? Who had left Hiko hanging? Why did Carrie, not Hiko, close the door? Carrie's response:

> It was my feelings that I left hanging. I had spoken to him on the phone, but I still had not expressed my feelings, those same feelings that I had left hanging many years before. I closed the door on my feelings now, just as I had ten years ago, when we

broke up. Talking to Hiko on the phone was an opening, but the issue was not resolved.

Carrie wrote Hiko a letter expressing the sadness and pain she had experienced when they originally separated, and suggested that they meet in person. Sick as she was, she offered to travel to meet him. Hiko's response was ambiguous. Carrie's grief turned to anger.

> I had been concerned that my thoughts of Hiko were a threat to my marriage. I tried to ignore them. Now I realize it was not that I still loved him, but that I loved him when we said good-bye. Those feelings had stayed frozen in time. Now those feelings were beginning to emerge.

The death of Carrie's grandmother, and the abrupt ending of the relationship with Hiko, were unresolved emotional issues—the "stuff" in her mouth on which she was choking. (Unprepared to face painful issues with her husband, she was soon to discover that these issues were adding to her suffocation.)

Paralleling her new-found emotional awareness, Carrie's relationship with the cancer continued to change.

> Over time, I began to understand the meaning of this question: What must I do to heal myself emotionally, psychologically and spiritually—whether I am cured of cancer or not? What do I need to change in my life so that I can live at peace with my inner self?

She longed for the cancer to leave, but it never left. Though the prognosis had been six months, she lived with it for six years, for she possessed a driving need to find the Hindu—to find her soul. We worked on many levels. But whether we addressed her relationships, or her buried emotions, her relationship to her cancer dominated. Initially, she feared to face it. But despite a death sentence (from the medical profession), and the resignation of family and friends, Carrie had the courage to proclaim, "I am going to live, *with* the cancer!"

After stopping chemotherapy (one and one-half years after her diagnosis), she enjoyed three good years in which she studied Tai Chi, Hatha Yoga, meditated, and even skied. She wrote a series of pamphlets for people diagnosed with cancer, and began to work on a book about her own experience. During this period, her consciousness changed; her focus shifted. No longer intent on eradicating the cancer, she embraced it as a vehicle for her transformation.

Carrie was continually plagued by the medical profession. Should she get a CT scan? Were the spots larger? Was there significant change? Had the number of sites increased? She faced devastation each time the doctor delivered his negative findings. Time and again she was pressured to resume chemotherapy— even though she knew she never would.

Exploring her relationship with the cancer, Carrie took a workshop on shamanism. Issues of *power* and *control* surfaced. Her understanding of the *difference* between them affected another major turning point. In the workshop, which focused on gaining personal power by accessing non-ordinary reality, Carrie discovered that her power animal was the sea turtle. This helped her open to a strength that had been long repressed.

We confronted the figure of cancer which continued to overwhelm her. I played the role of the cancer, saying, "It doesn't matter what you do, I will destroy you. I am more powerful than the whole medical establishment. What chance do you have against me?" Carrie could not face me. She dissolved into tears of hopelessness. Then, very gradually, she began to confront the powerful figure of cancer/death.

The interplay between her understanding of shamanism, our work with the figure of cancer/death and the last message from her oncologist (that her cancer was getting worse) forced her to contemplate the relationship between power and control. "How can I control my cancer, when I can't control my destiny?" She struggled with this question for months, carrying it like a Zen koan. During the shamanism workshop, she journeyed in search of her power animal. Discovery of a sea turtle recalled her knowledge of this particular species. After laying their eggs, this species swam for days without stopping. Even when barriers were placed in their path, the turtles kept swimming! If they stopped, they would not survive. They would be eaten by predators.

This made a deep impression on Carrie. She identified with the turtles' "soul driven" characteristics. "Despite all odds, I persisted, intuition my guide." Carrie's decision to stop chemotherapy, despite all medical warning, caused her to write:

> No one can control death, but I can empower myself to live *despite* a diagnosis of terminal cancer. No one around me, including the doctors, could be more powerful than my cancer. But *I* could! The power had to come from within me. Essentially, this is what happened to me. I stopped struggling with the question of how I could control my death. I began to control my life.

This breakthrough caused a shift in Carrie's awareness. She was released! She no longer felt powerless in the face of terminal illness.

What extended Carrie's life for six years? My intuition told me that the integral approach extended her life. One-pointedly she had set out, not to cure her cancer, but to *discover her soul.*

From the very beginning, she was intrigued by the Chinese approach to disease. She received acupuncture and acupressure, modalities using needles and finger pressure to remove blockages in the body's meridians. When this subtle energy flow is blocked, physical, emotional or mental dis-ease results. In China, this flow is called *chi*; in Japan, *ki*; and in India, *prana*. Trained as a scientist, Carrie was initially skeptical. However, we began to do process acupressure on a regular basis. Several dramatic experiences caused her to embrace *chi* as a reality.

During her first acupuncture treatment she had a vision of a narrow strip of light running up and down her body (primarily up and down her legs and chest to her neck). She attributed this to the drugs she was taking. This vision recurred many times, but she never spoke of it. Then, when she began acupressure treatments, the light grew. Though she mentioned it, she was not ready to explore it. Two months later, reading a book on Chinese medicine describing *chi*, realization came. "I was seeing my *chi* and didn't even know it!"

Subsequently, Carrie read that, when people are seriously ill, the life force is condensed into a narrow strip. Another confirmation! Slowly, the *chi* began to spread to other parts of her body. One day I asked her to draw a picture of what she saw. She drew the light coming from her feet, up through her legs into her chest and arms. (She did not, however, see the light entering her head. This worried her because lung cancer often metastasizes to the brain).

A few weeks later, as Carrie's acupuncturist manipulated her head and neck before inserting needles, "I suddenly saw a bolt of light go from my neck into my head and out the top." The acupuncturist *felt* what Carrie *saw*. This impressed her: Her *chi* was expanding.

Three months after her last chemotherapy treatment, Carrie was taking her daily walk when suddenly, "I had the image of a stream of white light going down my left arm. It started at a point near my heart or left lung, and traveled down my left arm into my index finger." She drew a picture of her experience, then put it away. For two weeks, she saw this image every time she walked. Then it faded away. She didn't mention it to her therapists, and eventually forgot it. Months later, she read a book with illustrations of the meridian pathways. The lung meridian looked like her drawing. She realized that she had seen her lung *chi*! She felt very empowered. After seeing three practitioners (who worked with subtle energy) on three successive days, Carrie had the following experience:

That night I was awakened by the feeling that my entire body was glowing. I felt that energy was radiating from me in every direction. It was a golden light which lasted for about fifteen minutes—a unique experience!

Five months after Carrie stopped chemotherapy, thoughts of her lost lung crept into her mind. The horror of two surgeries had created a repressed reservoir of trauma, grief and loss. Awareness of this loss emerged during an acupressure session with me. The image of lying on the operating table, doctors and nurses above her, manifested. It triggered an emotional deluge. We worked to release it for many months.

During this time, I taught Carrie *pranayama* (breathing techniques) to increase her lung's capacity. Focusing on her breath evoked images of the surgeries, and the emotions associated with them. Eventually Carrie was able to remember the state of the woman who had consented to the removal of her lung, and to forgive herself.

Final analysis of Carrie's Hindu dream centered around her relationship with her husband, Steven. A recurring dream: While he gazes out the window, Carrie is suffocating. Initially, this dream made no sense to her. Steven was very supportive during her treatments, mothering their two-year-old daughter, Nora, while personally attending to Carrie's needs. Why, then, was he not listening to her (in the dream)? Several years passed before we could work on this.

Cracks in her image of Steven surfaced, however, in the fourth year of cancer. She had emerged from the trauma of the surgery. She was enjoying a renewed feeling of well-being, examining her current work in the world, her roles as wife and mother, her spiritual quest. As life returned to a level of normalcy, friction appeared in her marital relationship. She realized that Steven "did not know who I had become, nor was he interested in finding out." Literally, he could not listen to her. He would change the subject, read the newspaper. She was pursuing

a new path while Steven wanted her to return to their old one—
one which Carrie was transcending. As a result, Carrie lost
interest in intimacy and Steven resented her rejection.

While he willingly had been her care-giver for the last four
years, he could not abide her new-found freedom. Her efforts to
engage him in anything psychological or spiritual only triggered
annoyance. He said, "You have too much mental baggage."
Eventually, their relationship reached a crisis. This terrified her.
The crisis grew. Steven told her that he hated "all the stuff about
health and healing" (thus revealing more about the schism between them than about health and healing).

Slowly, Carrie began to remember the times, before cancer,
when she had suffered from Steven's insensitivity. "Feelings of
despair had accumulated. I realized now that much of this despair
was due to Steven." One early experience was associated with a
miscarriage. At fourteen weeks she had begun to bleed. The
bleeding became profuse. Unfortunately, Steven, a veterinarian,
had evening appointments and despite repeated warnings, he did
not get Carrie to the doctor until he finished his work. Repressing
feelings of abandonment, Carrie blamed *herself* for not stressing
the seriousness of her condition. The resulting miscarriage had
deep emotional repercussions. Unable to express her resentment,
Carrie went to a psychologist. Steven did not go with her.

Another experience resurfaced. Six months before Carrie was
diagnosed with cancer, she contracted a severe case of pneumonia. After four days, she insisted on going home. Though Steven
knew she was not fully recovered, he expected her to take care of
their child. Feeling terribly guilty, she protested that she was still
too weak.

Beginning to understand the dream in which Steven ignored
her suffocation, more and more Carrie resented his insensitivity.

Even after their child was born, Carrie continued to admin-
ister Steven's animal hospital. "I was exhausted beyond com-
prehension, suffered from chronic sleep deprivation and was
extremely unhealthy, physically, mentally and emotionally."

Desperate, she pleaded with Steven. Refusing to see the severity of her suffering, he told her they both had to work. "He ignored my pain."

Carrie tried to excuse these incidents. "Just ignore these stories, they happened in the past. If I didn't tell Steven then, what right do I have to complain now?" Nevertheless, once again her quest for the truth burst through the barrier of her conditioning.

> Eventually, I realized that in addition to my need to examine the truth for my own healing, it was not fair for me to keep my feelings from Steven. My healing journey had caused him to feel rejected. He was right. I was rejecting him because I had been deeply hurt in the past; now I was hurting him. The only way to move forward in our lives was to bring all of this out. These experiences were the "stuff" in my mouth in the recurring dream.

I began to see Carrie and Steven together for therapy. We worked, intermittently, for about a year. Initially, both were afraid that they would hurt each other. Exhausted from being Carrie's primary support (for the last four years), hurt by her rejection, still he could not abandon his role as care-giver: He believed that Carrie was too vulnerable to withstand his negative feelings. Also admission of anger would have shattered his self image. More adept at expressing her feelings, nevertheless, Carrie constantly struggled against exposing Steven. The sessions exhausted her. We had to break for several weeks.

All efforts to reduce hostility over intimacy failed. Carrie was undergoing major transformation. Physical closeness, for her, was predicated on the need to be seen spiritually. She stated bluntly, "You can't have my body without my soul." Steven, on the other hand, needed warmth and closeness. For years, his life had been unbearably stressful. Care of Carrie and Nora was exacerbated by financial straits. His need was for intimacy. She refused it. Frustrated, he reacted by resisting Carrie's need for her soul. He was threatened by it. This dichotomy cut off any further deep interpersonal communication.

This was, perhaps, the most difficult relationship work I have ever done. It seemed to reach a point of no return. We continued to work sporadically until Carrie's death became imminent.

> It had become apparent that Steven and I had gone separate ways in dealing with the struggles of my illness. In our pre-cancer days, both Steven and I had coping strategies that included ignoring the bad things in life as a way of making them disappear: If you think positively and "hide" from reality, you will be okay. Since being told I had an incurable disease, this strategy no longer worked for me. When cancer is inside of you, there is no place to hide. Part of my ability to deal with my illness has come from facing it head on. This approach is still very new for me, but it is beginning to work. Steven, however, is still holding onto old ways of coping.

November of 1998, three years after stopping conventional treatments, Carrie contracted a life-threatening pneumonia. Feverish, too weak to get out of bed, she consented to a CT scan. It revealed not only the pneumonia, but a further spread of the cancer. (When Carrie's doctor showed the scan to a radiologist, he asked if the person was still alive.) Her family doctor urged her to begin chemotherapy again. She refused. Both the doctor and Steven thought she had less than three months to live.

I saw Carrie at her home on a daily basis for several weeks. Since she found it difficult to speak, most of our work centered on acupressure treatments of her lung meridian. Preparations were made to call in hospice; the family saw her as dying. After two weeks, though her fear was extreme, she began to recover. Harnessing all the knowledge she had gathered from living with cancer, she proclaimed, "Although I thought I might die, I continued to tell myself that no one knows the future. I also thought that what I did today would make a significant difference in my health."

During this period, Carrie decided to create and lead a healing ceremony. The main purpose—to share her sense of spiritual consciousness with family and friends. "Once again, it was my spiritual health that seemed paramount." Though living with death had led her to explore virgin territory, she had not shared any of her discoveries with those closest. She felt compelled before she died to communicate her "true inner self" to those she loved.

More than thirty people witnessed Carrie expressing her deepest beliefs about living and dying. "The healing ceremony was filled with tears and laughter and a tremendous sense of relief, renewal and empowerment." She continued teaching others about the interdependence of life and death until she left her body.

To everyone's amazement, Carrie temporarily recovered. In order to be closer to family, she moved into a new home with Steven and Nora, celebrated her fortieth and Nora's seventh birthday, and a momentous fifth anniversary of the cancer diagnosis. The severity of the pneumonia attack fueled Carrie's aspiration to understand the *purpose of her life*. This deep impulse, transcending her earlier focus on *eradicating* the cancer, remained in the forefront throughout her dying process.

> I know that the reason I am still alive is because of all the work I have done on my health—physically, mentally, emotionally and spiritually. But why have I been given this opportunity to go on with life when so many others have died? I feel this tremendous desire to explore more. I want to spend more time dealing with spiritual issues, learning how to incorporate them into my daily life.

After five years of doing battle with two major surgeries, chemotherapy and some of the deepest psychological work I have ever witnessed, Carrie fully opened the door to her soul. While those around her were obsessed with her demise, she was hewing new pathways.

Conventional boundaries of psychotherapy had faded. I traveled to Carrie's home for sessions lasting hours, playing the role of midwife, helping to birth her emerging inner being. We worked intensively on plans for her to go on retreat.

> During these five years I have changed tremendously. Although I have the same husband, daughter, mother, father, sister, I feel *I am a totally different person.* My view of life is different. My beliefs and my relationships are different.

Carrie made her first foray into an individual retreat. Steven drove her to an ashram. Once there, however, feelings of isolation and over-exertion created anxiety. She chose to return home.

Addressing her fear of not being able to breathe, Carrie attended two workshops: "Cancer as a Turning Point" and "Opening the Heart." She continued to counsel others suffering from cancer, working on her book, concluding her series of pamphlets on cancer, and creating a website to inform people of her strategies.

Although in 1999 she contracted several bad colds, plus another attack of pneumonia, she still pursued her inner work. "As I continue to acknowledge my soul, and live my life accordingly, I feel a new sense of inner peace." In contrast to religion, which sees "God" as external, she believed that spirituality came from within. "All things on earth possess a soul, and they are connected to each other through a spiritual energy."

She was aware now that her illness was directly connected with her purpose:

> I see my purpose in life, not so much to "be someone" (teacher, wife, mother), but, rather, to find my soul and to communicate to others the power of that center for healing.

For the third time, in December of 1999, Carrie contracted pneumonia. Until her death in August, she sensed its imminence.

"Six years of coughing, and several bouts with pneumonia, have taken their toll on my remaining lung." Preparing intensively for her exit, she attended a death and dying conference; she guided Nora toward acceptance, wrote letters to her (with instructions that they be opened at auspicious times in her life), read voluminously on the dying process. When she could no longer read, she listened to audiotapes and watched videos on spiritual practices. She continued to explore until her last breath.

By June, Carrie had to use oxygen nightly, lost interest in food and began to lose weight. Her biggest fear was suffocation.

> While some people might see our household as depressing, I see it as being filled with love and appreciation for each new day. We are living on a very different plane of existence than most people our age. Sometimes, I feel like I am watching a movie, and I just can't believe this is all really happening. But it is.

In the final two months of Carrie's life:
- She had accomplished her life purpose, i.e., to become fully aware of her soul.
- She experienced a fully conscious dying process.
- She served others by teaching them about soul and the dying process.

"The very cells of my body are collapsing. Why am I continuing to live?" I advised her to consult with the Hindu. The next day she murmured, "My soul said I need more time. I have to learn as much about the dying process as possible."

A month before her death Carrie called her family to her bedside. While grateful for the fine care she had received, she challenged them to go further.

> Taking care of me and comforting me are greatly appreciated. Being a participant in the process of my dying goes a step further. I am in a very different world than you. Consider entering my world.

She prepared six pages of instructions entitled "How to Share My Final Days in This Lifetime." Appended to these instructions were prayers and meditations to ease her passage.

> The following are suggestions for the final days before death, especially when I am no longer able to communicate verbally with you. I will be transitioning between two realms. In every crisis there is an opportunity. You can use this tremendous opportunity to help me cross into another plane of existence. Though the fear of the unknown can be great, I believe I will be entering a plane of existence that is filled with eternal light, eternal time. A place of total connectedness where All is One. You can help facilitate this great once-in-a-lifetime process:

1. **Sit in silence** with me, for as long as you would like. Time is limited for you, not me. I am already entering eternal time.
    Share the silence with me.
    Please, do not pity me.
    Do not assume I am suffering (unless I have obvious physical pain).
    Watch your own emotions and how you may project them on me.
    Share your love and compassion, not pity and fear during the silence of the final days.

2. **Speak to me softly** about whatever you want. Good things are preferable!
    I believe that the sense of hearing is the last sense to go. I may not respond but I may hear everything you say. I do believe that the last words I hear could be important in carrying me over to other planes of existence, so keep this in mind.
    I do believe it is necessary for me to separate emotionally from everyone around me in order to fully let go of this lifetime, so while your emotions may be running high, mine

may be declining, out of necessity, to enter another spiritual realm. You can remind me that it is okay to let go and to follow the light. My love will not be gone. It simply will not be attached to my body anymore. It will be to my benefit to detach emotionally more and more in the final days.

3. **Read any of the meditations/prayers** attached. You can read just one or many. Individual ones can be repeated many times. (There are no rules here.)

4. **Read the loving kindness (metta) meditation.** I first learned this from Joan Borysenko. It is an ancient meditative prayer. I know it will continue to be passed down through many generations. Nora already knows it.

5. **Feel free to touch me lightly,** especially my hands and feet. I imagine that I will still be comforted by a light foot rub up through the final days.

6. **Read with Nora, or any other children, the book, "What's Heaven?"**
    Read this book with them while sitting with me. It is a great way to include the children. They need to be included. The last few pages of the book are the best. Adults can read it alone, too. Cry with children. This is how they learn to grieve. They will thank you for it in the future.

7. **Special Considerations for Nora**
    Read with her the letter I wrote to her, with me there in the bedroom. She may not understand all the words, but she will clearly understand the feelings. (Remember, Steven, there are more letters for her in the bank safety deposit box. I believe they will be very important for her.)

8. Allow Nora to be with me anytime she wants, though she needs to be with me quietly. NEVER tell Nora she is

bothering me. Let her see me anytime and explain to her that I can no longer respond in the usual ways. DO NOT try to protect her from my death. See this as the ultimate way to teach her about death, the most natural and inevitable thing that occurs after birth. Support questions, but follow her lead. Do not, however, leave her in the room alone with me or ask her to take care of me in any way.

9. Do not turn on music or open window blinds. When a person is dying, the senses go inward. Outward senses are annoying distractions to the process. Please keep noise levels down as much as possible, including opening and closing closets and drawers.

10. My mantra has been:
"I honor the eternal light within me." I hope to continue saying this as I enter the next mystery. Feel free to repeat it for me, to remind me at any time. Also remind me to follow the light and that it is okay to let go.

11. Please call Arya for any other suggestions. I need him to help me in this great transition.

Reading these final instructions, I suddenly remembered a younger Carrie who, true to her scientific training, believed only in the visible world. Her journey had carried her beyond her conditioned personality to the realms of the transpersonal.

Twelve days before her death, Carrie wrote her own eulogy. She charged me with the responsibility, and honor, of reading it at her funeral. It stands as testimony to a radical transformation. This is what I read to family and friends at her funeral:

How could I leave this world without leaving all of you a letter? And how could I start my letter without an infamous quote?

"Tis better to have loved and lost.... Than never to have loved at all." (Alfred Lord Tennyson) The emotional pain is so intense only because the joys have been so great! Who am I who has died? You have lost your friend, your relative, your daughter, sister, wife, mother, or granddaughter. But for me I am losing all of you at one time. I am losing my child, my mother, father, sister, husband, dog, other relatives and friends, all in a single moment. Dwelling on the thought of that can be overwhelming, even overbearing! It is part of the ultimate lesson of living in the moment because the thought of losing everyone is really a "future" thought. This is, however, by far an extremely difficult task to live moment by moment. So for me I need to transcend the emotional pain of my losing all of you in order to die into a spiritual place of existence. It is this spiritual existence that I am looking ahead towards while leaving behind the emotional and physical pain.

Remember that I am filled with more love than you can imagine—it's just that my love is no longer attached to a physical body. It is eternal love. When you see turtles in a stream, leaf buds in the springtime, snowy hills in winter, or more, that is where I will be at home. I have no doubt you will feel my presence there and it will cause you to smile because you know I am in the world where everything is eternal.

Also, of course my love and spirit will get carried along into the many generations to come as well as everyone who has been touched by my life. Memories and stories and pictures get passed on long after the physical bodies. This is what spirit truly is. This is what gives life meaning.

I lived life more fully for the past six years than in the previous thirty-five years put together. Yes, I would have liked many more years, especially because of being a parent of a young child, but I was blessed with a wonderful forty-one years. The difference between forty-one and eighty-one is really nothing relative to eternal time. I could ask, "Why me?" in terms of why I was diagnosed with cancer at thirty-five-years-old, but I could also ask why I didn't die at thirty-six-years-old as the doctors predicted. Just a few days ago, I gave my Hospice nurse a set of my pamphlets. She told me she gave them to a cancer patient who then spent the last week of her life discussing them with her mother. They had meaningful life and death discussions during that last dying week. Without ever knowing who these people are, I felt as if my life had great meaning. This is one of many examples for me. I have accomplished so much, done so much, helped so many people in the last six years. Perhaps, this was the true purpose of my life. Ironically, I feel that everything I did was for myself. I wrote my pamphlets, created my web site, had healing ceremonies because I needed to do these things to help myself feel better. (I am not talking about curing cancer but about healing my inner self.) But there was a tremendous ripple effect that unintentionally affected so many people. It still astonishes me. If I had one bit of advice to pass on, this would be it: Take time to work on your own inner healing. It will automatically affect everyone else around you in a positive way.

In the book, *The Art of Dying,* the author presents a scenario. She said imagine that it is a time before you are born. You are in heaven (or whatever is a comfortable place), and an angel or messenger, if that sounds better, is giving everyone a piece of paper. It is your assignment for life on earth. You could choose to accept or decline it. Though it is a very difficult assignment, you choose to accept it because you know that life on earth is so precious. Now you have lived your life. You are about to die, looking back, would you have chosen to accept your assignment on earth? Think about it.

Despite the huge physical and emotional challenges of these past six years, despite dying at only forty-one-years-old and despite having to leave my daughter at such a young age to be raised by others, I would answer, "definitely yes." I would choose to do this again. The years have been precious to me. This answer actually brought me some sense of relief and comfort.

I am not angry at life. I do not see life as unfair (although there was a time when I was terribly angry over my cancer diagnosis). I do have deep sadness that I have to leave this wonderful, beautiful, miraculous world.

We don't know, of course, the details of death, but I believe the human being is composed of the body-mind-heart-soul. I have written them as one word because I believe they are intricately connected. Do they separate during the dying process or are they all so impermanent to begin with that they do not really separate? Perhaps, they separate on this plane of existence, but on other planes way beyond our understanding, they are all connected as One, One light, One eternal time. To get there, our emotional attachments on this earth are probably in the way and we must detach from them when we feel the body-mind start to shut down.

Stephen Levine wrote that when you touch pain with fear, it is pity. When you touch pain with love, it is compassion. Keep this in mind. The pain is impermanent and will not last forever. The fear and pity dwell on the past. Eventually, the love and the compassion shine through for eternity.

I really hope that no one refers to my life as having "struggled for six years with cancer" or "constantly fighting cancer" or worse yet "losing the battle with cancer." I developed a disease that is a mystery, complicated by many factors. But during these past six years I have accomplished so much, become the person I truly want to be, and I do not see myself as having lost anything. I have worked extensively on myself, learned amazing new things, met people I never would have met otherwise, extended what I have learned to so many people who have thanked me in so many ways, not to mention six years of sharing many memorable moments with my family. To say that I "lost" anything would simply be totally wrong.

I feel that I have been blessed with tremendous opportunities over my lifetime. And I am so grateful for the past six years.

I wish all of you the miraculous blessings of life that occur each and every day in the world. Just keep looking for them.

CHAPTER

6

Where Are My Children!

OPENING THE DOOR ... I find myself face to face with Joshua Callahan, new born, nestled on his mother's chest. Pushing a stroller, Patrick Callahan, the father, flashes a smile. Focusing on Joan's shining face, my mind traces the torturous route leading to this happy scene.

After graduating from college, Joan entered therapy in 1987. Her first utterance, "I don't know who I am," told me that her journey was to be one of self-discovery.

It took twelve years to realize this truth.

For two years we worked consistently on Joan's relationship with her parents, and with the men in her life. We confronted the issues that arose from living with a depressed mother and a verbally abusive father, their eventual divorce and her forced acceptance of the role of "mother" to her younger brother. However, this exploration did not lead us to the root cause of a life-long fear. Sobbing, she repeatedly voiced her dream: To have a child with a loving husband. As early as age eight, she wrote passionately in her journal about a child she longed for, but believed she could never have. Joan's story unfolded slowly.

In 1989, she moved from New York to Sitka, Alaska. On the night of her arrival, she walked into a bar and met John, the man with whom she would spend the next ten years. Instantly, she recognized him. When he left the bar, Joan followed. With uncharacteristic boldness, she asked, "Are you shy or are you married?" He said that he had been recently separated from his wife; then revealed that he had not left on his fishing boat that morning because he had "sensed" her arrival. However, he roughly warned her, "If we are to have a relationship, it will be good for me and bad for you. You will have to do *all* the giving."

Eventually, Joan was to endure the truth of his prophetic prediction.

When they parted that evening, Joan experienced a familiar panic attack. Separation from a loved one had always triggered the feeling that she was going to disappear. Though she had just met John, she suffered the familiar numb, tingling in her hands that accompanied separation. Sadness engulfed her after his departure, but instinctively she knew he would be an important part of her life.

Eventually she moved into his house—initiating a relationship that was to be filled with pain and frustration. Though she took care of John's two children, his ex-wife made all the decisions. Her sense of enslavement and John's depressed, passive-aggressive behavior imprisoned her.

I worked with Joan eight years, primarily via phone and letters. During her rare visits to New York, our work centered on her unhappy relationship. Yet always, in the end, she could not leave John. "Somehow, I have to make it right with him," she sobbed.

In August of 1997, Joan's ninth year with John, I received a letter from her, "Living with John is killing me. But I cannot leave." Desperate, she asked to visit me for prolonged, intensive therapy. She needed to know what strange attachment kept her tied to John. Though overwhelmed by grief, she was keenly aware of the deep schism in her life—strength and self-direction in her work as therapist, teacher and artist, yet utter helplessness in her relationship.

At the end of August, 1997, Joan arrived for our first three-day intensive, her leg infected, her feet covered with rashes, fungus and eczema. Once again, with a sense of powerlessness, she informed me that *she could not leave John.* Employing a series of gestalt exercises (in which role play evokes different parts of the personality), Joan contacted a part of herself which she identified as "cowboy." Though this inner figure gave her more freedom of expression, I sensed it would not solve her dilemma. I decided to use holotropic breathwork.

Created by Stanislav Grof, breathwork employs deep, rapid breathing. Utilizing music/sound played at extremely high volume, an altered state of consciousness is induced. Memory of one's personal/psychological history, of the time in the womb, even of the birth process itself may emerge, as well as mystical, shamanic, past-life or near-death experiences. The following sessions revealed past-life stories, containing characters Joan had never met, in settings far removed from her own life experience. Leading her far beyond her conditioned reality, holotropic breathwork allowed Joan to glimpse, for the first time, the *source* of her suffering.

After five minutes of deep breathing, she shouted in a strong African accent, "Where are my children?" Two hours of perpetual movement (involving arms, legs, pelvis, shoulders, head) followed, accompanied by an overwhelming anger, grief and terror. Awestruck, I witnessed the transformation of a white woman raised in New York City into a black woman from a primitive village in Africa.

Shrieking with agony, reliving the loss of her children, she stood up, "beat" a drum, tore at her hair, begged to die and berated herself for being a bad mother. Entranced, she maintained intense movement and feeling for two hours.

At the end of the session, shaken by her own experience, Joan related the following:

> I am a black woman living in a small village in Africa. I see my surroundings clearly and am immediately aware of grief and terror coursing through my body as I search for my three

children. Again and again I shout, 'Where are my children? Did
you see my children?' As I run along the dirt paths, I am aware
that a stampede of wild elephants is headed for our village. We
must leave or be trampled. My ten-year-old son, my six-year-
old son and three-year-old daughter are nowhere to be found
and I am faced with a terrible choice—leave without my children or be killed.

Ultimately, I am forced to leave with the other villagers,
never having found my children, never knowing if they were
alive or dead. Now I am on a dirt road beating my drum, calling,
"We are leaving, where are you, my children?" Panic invades
me. My feet and legs feel hollow. I can see my slender body, my
long legs and arms, the pale palms of my hands and soles of my
feet. I wear a brown fabric wrap and a short necklace of large,
amber-colored beads. My hair is closely cropped. I cannot
forgive myself for leaving. I should have stayed to be killed with
my children. I imagine my eldest son returning to find his
mother gone. I would rather he found me dead. Oh! What kind
of a mother am I?

For many years, I play out my role in the community, but I
am not alive inside. Repeatedly, I cry out to God, "I wish I had
died instead of my children!" Standing in front of our hut, I vow
that I will find my eldest son. I vow that I will never leave him
again. *I vow that I will never leave anyone again!*

I wait to die and finally see myself dead, floating on the
water in a wicker/straw casket. I am lying on my back and see
my hands with their long, thin fingers folded across my chest.
Suddenly, I see a (white) brightness above me and I slip out of
my body. I look down at myself floating on the water and repeat
over and over, "I will never forget my children. *I will never leave
anyone again.*" My eldest boy's face appears. I tell him how
much I love him, that I will never leave him again.

Near the end of the session, as I open my arms to embrace
him, I suddenly feel the spirit of my *child-to-be* and realize that
there is no room for him in my present life. A profound "no!"
arises from within. I cannot betray my first son again. If I let this
new child in, I will lose my boy. I am very confused.

I experience great compassion for the African woman (who is myself). But since she-I has not forgiven herself, what can I do in order to have a child in this life?

On the third and final day of our first intensive, Joan and I gathered together emerging threads of insight. Reminding her of her *present* dilemma (of living with a man who did not want any more children) Joan cried, "I am in this relationship not because I want to stay, but because I *cannot* leave!" Using process acupressure during this session, I watched as her story emerged. Suddenly, reverting to her fear of having a child, Joan experienced a spontaneous vision of her oldest African son.

Returning swiftly to her life as an African woman, she once again relived the crying, pleading and apologizing. This time, however, she not only identified with, but was *witness* to the African mother's intense pain. This observation allowed her to bridge the relationship between the two lives.

Realizing that the African mother's guilt strongly negated her desire to have a child, Joan envisioned the African mother and her three children. "This is our story," she tells them. "There is a white woman in a different lifetime who wants to have a child. This woman can be mother to you." The oldest boy, however, resisted.

Trapped between two worlds, both Joan and the African woman could not evolve until Joan admitted her fear. Despite her desire to bear a child, she was terrified of conception. In an imaginal dialogue with her African counterpart, Joan said: "I am weak. I can't do it." Calmly, the African woman replied, "You are strong. You will be a good mother. I choose you!" At these words Joan, too, became calm. "You are right!" she cried. "Allow *me* to be mother now! Forgive yourself and set us both free!"

Smiling, she told me:

As I let go of my fear, I saw the African mother's transparency enter into me! I have become the major figure.

Joan left our three-day intensive awed by the depth of her experience: Armed with new understanding, she returned to Sitka. Although apprehensive, she revealed everything to her partner.

> I told John about Africa, holotropic breathwork, process acupressure and souls. He listened intently, asked for details. Shedding tears, he reminded me of our uncanny recognition upon meeting. He talked of a "great white light" he had seen as a child.
>
> I was flooded with feeling: Could it be that he was my eldest African son? Though he could not remember that other life, I begged his forgiveness; I spoke to his soul, not to his personality.

By entering a past life, Joan recognized a character with whom she identified and a character who she recognized. Although psychologists like Roberto Assagioli theorize about sub-personalities, Western psychology speaks of each individual having *one* personality. Deviations are seen as pathological manifestations of an alternate personality or dissociation from the sense of self. In Joan's case, healing demanded the accessing of various personalities and relationships from different lifetimes. Carrying the personality of the African woman, she unconsciously created an obstacle to childbirth. When she entered into a relationship with her, she removed the obstacle.

Joan's story is not one of severe sexual or physical abuse, nor is it one of intense spiritual opening. It is the story of a woman seeking relationship and motherhood and how her life intersects with the transpersonal.

After our first intensive session, Joan's hopes about a life with John had been re-kindled. Four months later, however, old patterns resurfaced. She returned to continue our work. As in our first intensive, she *adamantly* refused to leave John. "I owe him. I am responsible for him." But Joan had achieved greater clarity. Tracking her own process through dreams and synchronicities, she recalled the strange connection she had with her first love, Patrick Callahan. They had met when she was seventeen. "No one ever loved me so deeply." When she left for college, Patrick gallantly told her that he loved her, but she was not to feel guilty if she dated others. A year later, she broke his heart. For seven years, however, they kept in contact.

In her first dream, she saw Patrick on a bus with two children. She sensed that he was unmarried but wondered to whom the children belonged. Waking, she noted the time was 3:45 A.M. Checking her answering machine in the morning she heard Patrick's voice. Her surprise deepened when he said, "The time in New York is 7:45 A.M."

In December 1997, Joan had a second dream in which Patrick urged John to end his relationship with Joan: *He* is the one who can offer her love, marriage and children. Upon waking, Joan again received a phone call from Patrick. This time, she answered. In their conversation, he revealed the complexity of his life. He has fathered two children from two different women and though his relations with the women were over, his obligations to his children continued. He urged her, "Come back to New York. Marry me. I have a house and garden. We'll have children together."

With this in the background, our second intensive session commenced. Again she returned to her African lifetime. Speaking in strong dialect, she pleaded with her elder son for forgiveness: As I encouraged her to let him go, familiar separation symptoms surfaced—panic, pain, intense tingling in her hands, but for the first time realization flooded her. She understood that *she* was holding *him* captive. As her sobs diminished, she cried, "You are free! Live your own life now!" Her left hand clasped her shirt. As I applied pressure to this hand, I asked, "Is this where you keep your children?" Relief pervaded her body. As she removed her hand, she said, "Now I will have a baby. My African children will live in this child."

Imaginally, she returned to the dirt road in Africa—her legs and feet, however, no longer felt hollow. "Bright, flashing, white lights circle my head!" she cried. Though she continued to communicate with the African woman, this session liberated her from the trauma of her past lifetime.

The synchronicity of Joan's dreams and Patrick's telephone calls at last broke a ten-year pattern of frustration. On the third and final day of our intensive, Joan's underlying anger surfaced. She explored similarities between her mother and John, "I can't trust either of them. *I can't trust anyone!*" Lack of trust now became our major theme. During process acupressure, Joan moved from a mental to an imaginal level: "A blue-green egg covers my womb. It is my shield." "Can you imagine removing that shield?" "Only for Patrick. He is the *only one I trust.*"

After leaving, Joan called Patrick to probe his dilemma. Despite this entanglement, Joan knew that she wanted to see him again but she needed to end her relationship with John.

She returned to Sitka apprehensive, but determined. Thus began the process of separation. Within a month Joan left John and flew back to Patrick in New York. Now, however, Patrick became ambivalent—resurrecting their relationship meant facing the wounds of the past and the reality of the present. Once again Joan would be the outsider, but this time she would have to deal with two hostile mothers and their children. The strength of Joan's and Patrick's connection was more powerful than their difficulties, however, and they married with hopes of having a family together.

After their marriage, Joan returned for holotropic work. In this session she entered another past life in which she saw herself as an Egyptian dancer. Embroiled in jealousy and intrigue, she became acutely aware of her present situation and her confusion about mothering children who were not her own. As a result of this journey she better understood the mine-field surrounding her.

She returned in early November, 1999, for her last holotropic experience *before* conceiving. Here is her account:

> I began my last session with continuing memories of children
> lost. Flashes of light were accompanied by the familiar torture
> in my chest. Experiencing the pang of losing child after child (in
> different lifetimes), I actually saw their faces! I called out their
> names. When the African woman appeared, I begged her for
> help. Intuitively, I knew that a woman from my Egyptian birth
> would sabotage me. Once again, I re-lived the Egyptian lifetime.
> I experienced myself as Joan, lowering the Egyptian woman
> into a coffin. I said good-bye. Now the African woman became
> my guide. "Trust and love your husband," she said, "Take care
> of your feet." When I lost my African children, I lost all feeling
> in my feet and legs. In this lifetime, they have been covered with
> eczema, psoriasis and fungus—which cleared up after I left
> John. Opening my eyes, I knew for the first time that I would
> have children.

Joan went home, strong and confident. A few weeks later in
December, she discovered that she was pregnant! Though Joan
accessed vital information from past births, a philosophical/
spiritual belief in reincarnation is *not* necessary for healing to
occur. Whether viewed as stories from the unconscious, or as past
lives, the effect is the same.

A psychology honoring the soul as the center of the being
reveals both the African woman and the Egyptian dancer as
vehicles manifesting the *one* soul.

> Man is in his self a unique Person, but he is also in his
> manifestation of self a multi-person; he will never succeed in
> being master of himself until the Person imposes itself on his
> multi-personality and governs it.... (Sri Aurobindo, 1987, pp.
> 897-98)

From this perspective, Joan's past-life exploration illustrates the effect of multi-personality manifesting in the service of the One Person.

Postscript

The interfacing of personal and transpersonal material in psychotherapeutic work often opens several routes for healing. The work of clearing personal history prepares the way for the manifestation of the transpersonal dimension of psyche. Or, the emergence of the transpersonal can ease the work on personality. Joan's work of clearing the transpersonal trauma opened the way for Joshua's birth. However, his birth set the stage for confronting the trauma of her own childhood. Prior to her past-life realization these experiences had remained hidden. As a mother she stepped into a constellation of people and events that replicated her early life: a house in the suburbs, an absent husband, isolation, two angry women and fear of being alone with a baby.

Plagued by panic attacks whenever Patrick left the house, Joan returned to therapy. Following the process of the panic, she remembered being left with her depressed mother and younger brother; Joan was five, Eric, three. Her father's departures set her on a survival course. How could she control both her brother's and her own behavior so as not to disturb her mother, who beyond periodic trips to the kitchen for vodka refills, spent her days in a darkened bedroom. Any noise sent her into uncontrollable rage.

Joan's strategies to keep the beast at bay included playing *quietly* with Eric in her room, taking him outside, and entertaining him in the family car. Her mothering of Eric paralleled her mothering of Joshua once her husband left for work. In a state of terror Joan fled with Joshua, driving aimlessly until Patrick returned.

Then, one day, in therapy, Joan contacted the source of her trauma. She recalled playing in the car with her brother, when her crazed mother suddenly appeared. Regressing to age five, Joan whispered, "Shh, Shh. Eric, get down ... hide! No! Mommy, no, no....!" Screaming and flailing, she curled into the fetal position, clutching her throat and gasping for breath.

This was the beginning of accessing several traumas in which Joan had nearly died. During these attacks Joan left her body. "But I had to return," she said, "for my brother's sake."

Joan made connections necessary for her healing that were both personal and transpersonal. Her desire to consciously mother the child she so longed for led her on a journey which helped her discover the root causes of her behavior.

CHAPTER

7

Transforming Torture

Will you forgive me for making literal an experience that seems
    more real than life, less possible than death?
There is no place to put it, no way to hold it, nothing to know
    it with.
And yet it belongs, it stays, and it begs consciousness...
(*My Heart*, unpublished poem)

JULIA'S WORDS REFLECT HER MYTHIC JOURNEY between heaven and
hell. Because the threads of her life's tapestry originate in the
underworld *and* the transcendental realms, this story of both
torture and of a soul's reclamation demands a new, extended
paradigm of the psyche: This paradigm gives width and breadth
to an experience that could be mis-diagnosed as *delusional* or
psychotic. Her process of self-awareness takes her deeper and
deeper into hellish realms of abuse before a turn-around occurs.
Gradually, however, her own experience of truth expiates her.

Julia interviewed me several times by phone before we met. I
sensed a woman on the edge of either radical change, or of
surrender to fear. Her mind, lucid and large, probed my experience, my training, my understanding of sexual abuse and *normal*
sexual development. The depth of her questioning rose, not from
curiosity, but from desperation. I passed the test and we sched-
uled our first session.

131

Verbally facile, Julia described in precise detail her past life with her family of origin; her present life in which she suffered from fear of intimacy with her husband; and her past confusing experience in therapy. Three themes dominated our initial work: sexual abuse by her older sister from age nine to eleven, beatings by her father from age three to twelve, and the confusion caused by her last therapist who actually *programmed* his clients to believe that they were sexually abused.

None of Julia's previous therapists focused on the trauma suffered as a result of abuse by her sister. When she related her experience with her sister, her last therapist immediately assumed that it was her *father* who had abused her, even going as far as to introduce images of sexual acts with him. Though disturbed by her sister's behavior, Julia became confused. Were her sister's explorations a *normal* part of sexual development?

Our work of bringing the traumatic impact of buried memories into consciousness began at our second meeting. Keenly aware of Julia's experience of *implanted* memories, I decided to work through the body, using process acupressure. The first manipulation of extending her legs triggered a violent shaking throughout Julia's body. This body memory helped her access further sensory channels. Slowly, she began to *visually* remember sexual play with her sister. *Proprioceptively,* she felt both the sexual stimulation and the physical revulsion. Once again she heard her sister's seductive call. Though dreading what would ensue, she could not say no. In a family devoid of affection, she had longed for physical intimacy.

Because of the intensity of the surfacing trauma, we had to extend the length of our sessions to two hours twice weekly, continuing this for two years. While we did not always use process acupressure, we always followed Julia's bodily signals. These took many forms—pain beneath the shoulder blade, heat throughout the spine, dizziness, trembling.... As we amplified each signal, long-forgotten parts of Julia's story steadily emerged.

While Julia had been *mentally* aware of her sexual abuse, until now she remained unconscious of her physical/emotional trauma. Gradually she allowed the fear, sadness and shame to enter her awareness. With this release came greater mental clarity.

Obsessively staging sexual roles, Julia's sister had assigned Julia the role of the man: She had to admire, touch, smell and taste different parts of her sister's body. As Julia now became conscious of the part she had been forced to play, physical revulsion and nausea flooded her. She began to connect her early conditioning with the pain of later sexual relationships.

Julia's therapeutic process was intense and layered. The incestuous relationship with her sister had inflicted a deep wound, but a deeper wound proved to be *even more severe*. What surfaced next was recall of physical abuse by her father.

Cultured and highly educated, an engineer, Julia's father wanted his children to experience the "finer things of life." A lover of music, he pressed them to study violin, demanding perfection at every step. They also swam competitively, their father at pool side, stopwatch in hand. Julia studied ballet and was taken to museums and concerts regularly by her parents. They were an upper-middle class, intellectual, Jewish family. This was the face presented to the world—the face held in Julia's *conscious* mind.

One of the many deep flaws in this family portrait was the father's terrible rage. For nine years he poured this rage into Julia, claiming that she was a "willful child" who needed discipline. In an explosive emergence of awareness Julia recalled her capacity to leave her body and enter other bodies. As we worked to release this new energy, she could no longer remain on the massage table. Needing room to writhe and cower and groan as she relived her father's wanton blows, she often appeared a crazed animal struggling for her very existence:

When I swam around the inner cells,
Moved through blood, entered bones
Passed through skin to inhabit the bodies of others,
I survived.
I left my own unprotected shell, organs exposed
Frightened by frequent blows
Raging energy propelled me out
Thrusting me from my skin, my bones, my cells
Shooting through my spine, amplified
Snapping it like a tree in a hurricane
Shattering it with currents of unimaginable sensation. (*Green*, unpublished poem)

A force *beyond* her sister's incest and her father's brutality was now present—a force so dark and overwhelming that it drove her out of her body. *We were entering the transpersonal realm.*

Julia began to *remember* leaving her body during times of abuse and assault and *re-experienced* this during our sessions. Mainstream psychology would not recognize the possibility of this phenomenon. The vast majority of psychologists would label this mode of survival as *delusional, dissociative* or *psychotic.*

Working with many trauma victims over the years, I have recognized two main modes of survival. One in which the consciousness remains within the body as it escapes into another part of the mind or personality. (If the trauma is severe, this strategy can create multiple personality or dissociative disorder.) Another in which the victim survives by *leaving the body.* This understanding of consciousness being projected outside of the body has been researched extensively by Kenneth Ring whose data revealed what he termed the *near-death experience.* Julia protected herself by leaving her body.

Julia's memory of these monstrous attacks heightened her awareness of *color.* She perceived her father's enraged energy in colors (hot pink and black). Other colors like yellow and green provided refuge.

His was an ugly, raging hot pink, coated sharply in thinly
outlined black
An inflamed vein of hatred, he sent into my small body
When he beat me with his open hand
Bone edges hard, flesh smoldering, capillaries enlarged.
(*Wrenching*, unpublished poem)

During our work, Julia's spine became a barometer. Heat and
sensitivity signaled the approach of dangerous forces. Too much
force propelled her out of her body; a very delicate balance
existed between her journeys to the dark side and the conscious
world. She proceeded with great caution. "Will it ever be safe to
fully occupy my body? Will I ever be able to trust another human
being?"

Descending still deeper into the long-sealed corridors of her
past, the reality of sexual abuse surfaced. Confused by the
manipulative nature of her previous therapy, she doubted the
veracity of incest images which were predominantly *mental*.

I steered clear of initiating exploration of incest with her
father, until one day the violence of his beatings was replaced by
the violence of rape. Julia tried to ignore the first influx of
images; but she suffered such visceral repercussions that she
could not dismiss them. Often they bypassed her visual perception, arriving somatically—revulsion, shame, need and sexual
arousal.

Can we create a universe not adverse to my speaking
Can we call up, evoke a goddess
Who can spread her transparent, finely-patterned cape
    sheer as a veil, around me
Expansively casting over us
A gentle epidermis of acceptance. (*Taken*, unpublished poem)

Breaking the secrecy, a conditioning that insulated the family,
was a formidable task.

Say, "He,
He touched me,
He used his mouth
He entered me and that was not enough
    in his torpid eyes
He laid his mouth upon my breast
So new, made so old
Woven of confusing veins" (*Taken*, unpublished poem)

At age twelve Julia confronted her father and the beatings stopped. However, two years later, after her older sister graduated and left home, her father's violence returned in the form of rape. She was victimized until she went to college at age eighteen.

Julia continued to question whether she was creating this rape in her mind. Her body, however, remembered that the violence with which he raped her paralleled the violence of his beatings. So intense was the energy in her spine during these assaults, that she imagined he had connected her to an electrical device. Although Julia's spine was strongly activated during these remembered rapes, she could no longer leave her body through this conduit. Instead, she escaped by entering patterns in the rug, a painting, a tree. She also entered her father's body. Here she experienced energetically his twisted, poisonous rage. Virtually devoid of feeling, like most sadists, he could evoke emotion only through violence. Hurting Julia had unleashed his sexuality.

Julia had yet to confront her most devastating demon. Painfully aware of the roles of her colluding sister and brutal father, she questioned, where her mother had been during this long, incestuous drama.

Descent to the primal depths of Julia's torture was initiated in a process acupressure session. As she recalled a group of people surrounding her, a sharp pain shot through her vagina. She was lying naked on a table while a woman inserted a metal object. Julia identified this woman as her paternal grandmother. Her father was also present. As this bodily sensation and the visual memory coincided, her back arched and her entire body lurched backwards. If I had not been there to catch her, she would have catapulted onto the floor. As I eased her to the ground, her body alternated between quaking and spasm. She lunged around the room trying to find asylum. Finally, she gripped me fiercely.

Julia had lifted a corner of the veil concealing a chaotic world of evil she had never imagined. Deeply shaken, she retreated to the safety of her rational mind. For several weeks we consciously avoided accessing the unconscious.

Ready to work at this deeper level, I decided to use holotropic breathwork. The gestalt of reclining on pillows while I watched her breathe recalled something familiar to Julia. She propelled herself backwards, as if to escape a pursuing force, slid across the floor and, curling into the fetal position, pressed her back against the wall. Repeatedly, she re-traced this pattern.

The force of the loud music as I witnessed her proscribed breathing had been overwhelming. Suddenly, she remembered a group of people gathered round her like sexual vultures. After this session Julia became very angry. She blamed me for subjecting her to "being watched." She blamed me for subjecting her to holotropic breathwork. Processing this anger for many weeks, we sorted out feelings of betrayal. Ultimately, Julia's healing process was served.

Her growing awareness of abusers beyond her sister and father triggered further realizations. She began to understand her fear of group participation. Though trained as a dancer, Julia could not tolerate being viewed while performing. As a result, she had not danced for years. As we uncovered details of group abuse, she began to dance by herself. Armed with a portable CD player and headphones, she discovered secluded meadows where her only audience was trees and sky. There she began to recover further opening into the world of spirit.

The contact I receive when dancing is ... I am graced by presence, presence of beings, guides, voices to lead me, to bathe me in divine grace, in beauty—it is nature, sun, air, insects, light, sky and clouds. And it is the very soil, solid ground on which I stand and then move to step and swing and turn and lean into air and fall back into sky—and dance with the goddess in love and joy and the sorrowful sadness that I am and have been for so long.

Julia's return to dance became a spiritual path, a way to heal. However, psychological recovery and discovery occurred simultaneously.

The entry of Julia's controlling mother into her story intensified our work. While they had done battle all her life, Julia dearly loved her mother and sought to protect her. Having contracted cancer when Julia was a toddler, she used her illness to manipulate the family. Though she forbade her family to speak of her condition, Julia was consumed with worry. Her mother's disease served another purpose, however. It obstructed a more pervasive family disease—*abuse*.

Julia's life-long efforts to protect her mother were not reciprocated. Her daughter's pleas for protection were met with graphic stories of beatings she had received when she was a child. Her constant refrain: "I had it much worse than you."

Suddenly, during a process acupressure session, Julia at last perceived her mother's involvement in the ritualized abuse:

We are in the basement of my childhood home. My father has me bent backwards on the ping pong table. He is raping me. Bright lights are shining in my eyes. My uncle is watching and my mother comes down the stairs with a knife.

This level of terror overwhelmed Julia. This descent from sexual abuse, beatings and rape, to group sex left Julia with no ground to stand on. "Am I crazy? My story is far too bizarre to be true!"

Face to face with her mother as madwoman, Julia needed a cognitive framework. I decided to explore her mother's family of origin. Her mother's paternal family had been orthodox Jews.

She too had been beaten by *her* father and older brother. Although Julia's mother was not religious and presented a highly rational exterior, she sometimes quoted the Old Testament scriptures. These passages arose and were delivered in a deep male voice as if another personality had rushed forward. Both Julia and her sister were disturbed by these eruptions—a bizarre juxtaposition to their mother's atheism. Equally bizarre was the relationship between her mother and uncle. Her mother deferred to and adulated her domineering and condescending brother. Julia's experience of her uncle utterly confused her. He fawned over her in early childhood, feeding the family myth of "Julia, the strongest girl in the world." During her teenage years, however, he periodically shamed her until she felt worthless. Though the puzzle of her mother's life remained a mystery, she became aware of the confusing and detrimental triangulation she experienced with her mother and uncle.

With a renewed aspiration for truth, she again plunged into the hidden world. Now she was guided by a strong bodily symptom—a sharp pain under her right shoulder blade. Simply placing my hand there facilitated her descent to yet another level of chaos—a chaos created by her mother and uncle.

Julia's body became incredibly rigid followed by violent shaking. Periodically, she attempted to escape by pushing backwards until she was sitting on top of the couch's back support. Screaming and moaning, she held on to me in a vice-like grip. After thirty minutes this struggle ceased and she became very quiet, resting in this space for another thirty minutes. Later, she described her experience:

> I am lying naked on a slab of marble before an ornately carved altar. A Dark One, my uncle worships, is present. My uncle sits me up and holds me while my mother cuts me under the right shoulder blade. She catches my blood in a vessel. A small dog laps the liquid. Then, she gives me to my uncle as an offering, and gives my blood to the Dark One.

As a child of four, Julia met the reality of evil, a reality she met many times on her journey with these strange people. This contact with ritualized abuse soon became dream-like. "How is it possible? Not my family!" In trauma work this need to distance is crucial, lest the victim be consumed in the horror.

Each time Julia re-visited this darkness, a similar pattern ensued: *a struggle, then quiet.* One day, during the quiet, she described a beautiful woman, gentle yet powerful, who came and took her to the "Other Place." She called her *the goddess, the Divine Mother.* After repeated visitations during her travail, Julia realized she could not have survived this darkness without Her.

> ... She took me to that Other Place: calm, beautiful, quiet—where I float and am free from the abuse. She is the essence of the Feminine ... touches me with the most loving touch ... lifts me and flies me away. She came to get me. I couldn't leave by myself.

At this young age the combination of her father's brutality and the ritualized torture demanded a powerful, loving intervention; anything less might have condemned Julia to either death or insanity. These appearances of Julia's Divine Mother in our work led to an ongoing relationship with a higher power whose presence evoked trust. Eventually, she no longer needed the stimulus of crisis to call forth the goddess. She appeared in her multitude of forms and conveyed her power in the joy of dance:

> ... I am totally connected to a power that is good and strong in earth and wind and sun. I dance in this place and the grass rises to meet me. The mountain towers before me, up the hill it rises and I move amongst ... nature's creatures who dart in and out. I speak to the trees and the hedges embrace me. I am one with all these forces ... feeling the messages come down through my arms, into my core, up through the soil and into my hips, through the very pores of my skin as I open to the blissful ease of moving in my own dance—given to me by the goddess.

Fortified and renewed by these contacts, Julia continued to expand her awareness of the underworld. Further exploration of the early ritual abuse revealed the torture and death of animals. Julia's terror and revulsion was accompanied by a deep compassion and fellow-feeling for these creatures. Gazing into their eyes, she realized their commonality of soul before their tormenters' soul-less forms.

Touching the grisly details of the animal sacrifices and her identification with them provided a launching pad for galactic travel. Julia rushed through her spine, out the top of her head "... into dimensions so far beyond human capacity ... star years, galaxies, huge space, a void." One day, after taking this escape route, she experienced great difficulty returning. Guiding her to a sand tray, I encouraged her to bury her hands; this helped her re-enter her body.

After numerous instances, she was adept at leaving her body, Julia announced that she wanted to stay in her human form. *She had a work to do on the earth and she wanted to experience loving relationships.*

> I traveled out so far into the galaxy, I became a star. I went light years out and yet, for the first time, I wanted to come back. I didn't want to explode like a star, lose form, never be in a human body again. I asked to return.

Julia's realization and choice marked *the major turning point in her work*: to choose life in a body, in a mind that had been so tortured. Paradoxically, uncovering the dark side had led her beyond shame and self-loathing to the discovery of her gifts, her essential core.

Realization of these gifts came one evening while giving her daughter a bath. Julia stretched out on the floor and gazed out the window:

> Suddenly, I realized, I just went into a tree. I do this; I go into trees; I move between and into other dimensions. I exist on

many more levels besides the concrete, the rational. My image
of myself and my attachment to it is dissolving as I allow these
powerful aspects of myself to emerge. I cannot deny them—*my
time traveling; my out-of-body experiences; my transpersonal
contacts with other beings; my receiving messages from other
realms—my existence on subtler levels.*

Julia's ever deepening excavations eventually brought her to
full awareness of her essence, her "...deep connection to forces—
light and dark, beautiful and divine, healing and powerful,
truthful and strong."

*   *   *   *

Julia and I created a sacred space, a space both free and
protected, where her story could safely unfold. Besides extended
therapy sessions, she wrote prolifically. Using her writing as a
means of connecting to herself and communicating with me, Julia
kept an extensive journal and created a large body of work with
her poems. The shame and revulsion, too terrible to utter, were
conveyed poetically. She began the awesome work of rebuilding
relationships by expressing her most intimate thoughts. Unveil-
ing the battle of her early life, she recovered parts of self crucial
to her search for wholeness—parts often identified with heaven
and hell. Again and again she entered the dark recesses of the
underworld, discovering not only the origin of her trauma, but
the power to heal it. Like the archetypal journey of the hero/
heroine, the woman who returned had undergone a radical
transformation. *Now*, the work of integrating this new self into
her present life would begin.

Julia had to sever many relationships in her battle for soul:
her sister and father, neither of whom could face her terrible
truth; several women friends who abandoned her in the worst of
times. Julia's mother had died several years prior to our work.
Still shaken from her dark passage, she stood naked before the
awesome work of re-creating her life.

Bearing open wounds of sexual violation, Julia dared to move towards her husband. Longing for an intimacy they had not known, she shared her most humiliating discoveries—opening to him amidst intrusive phantoms of the past. Discovering a balance was precarious; a moment of tenderness was often followed by weeks of estrangement. A work of this magnitude proceeds only through deep love and perseverance. Rather than focusing on lofty goals, she learned to focus on the *process*—finding joy in small gains.

Julia's relationship with her daughter revealed the highest levels of love, nurturing and care. She embodied the archetypal essence of *mother*, and yet could not shield her child from the fear that held her prisoner. Confronting her own fear helped her address her over-protectiveness. This ranged from mistrusting her husband's care to her own exhaustion from years of over-zealous attention to her daughter. True to her warrior spirit, Julia quickly acted to change the skewed family dynamics.

Julia's life-long search for Divinity in the form of the feminine rose with a renewed fierceness. Her relationship with the Divine Mother continued in ritual, dance and everyday spirituality. This inner connection has amplified her movement towards other women. Terrified of intimacy with women because of her mother's and sister's betrayal, she adopted the role of caretaker rather than friend in feminine relationships. Now, possessing a new awareness and strength, she is confronting this fear on many different levels. The most direct mode of confrontation lies in the telling of her story—an action that would have earned her torture or death in her childhood. A participant in a group of female trauma survivors, Julia has practiced sharing her truth, and has been received with great care and compassion. This vehicle, coupled with her strong aspiration for authentic relationship, continues to open new doors with women.

Julia looks upon the world with unveiled eyes. Her family of origin is gone and many illusions about her identity are also gone. Once familiar ways of perceiving herself and her world have changed. She has gazed into the eyes of death. She has gazed into the eyes of evil. But though she was forced into a world of fear and evil, she has received the touch of a divine, feminine presence she holds sacred and who, in turn, holds her sacred. Julia now possesses a radically different experience of *reality*; a battle-ground for light and dark forces:

> My precarious, precious life
> Given to me in trust by the Goddess
> Was quickly torn asunder, not by blunder, by forces wrenching
> Creating intentional tears, much harsher than broken threads.
>
> Deep within, my soul was called upon early
> To meet an evil maker
> The destroyer of hearts
> Dark beings that wind their way through the universe looking
> for a warm seat.
>
> At some point yet unrevealed
> My biological family
> Welcomed these unholy forces
> Into our artfully decorated house.
>
> How many generations back from what dark region of our
> Jewish past
> These seething multi-limbed entities came
> I cannot trace.
> I only know they lived in my childhood home.
>
> Amongst the Danish modern furniture of our living room
> Upstairs in the closely situated bedrooms
> Downstairs in the fluorescent lit ping-pong table basement
> Like they owned the property.
>
> How the malignant gray energy matter manifested
> In each of my assimilated relations

Was distinct
And corrupt. (*Wrenching*, unpublished poem)

Julia's life reveals an interwoven fabric of personal and transpersonal realities. She learned very early that human incarnation conferred the *power of choice*. Her family of origin welcomed "unholy forces" into their midst, and intentionally coerced her to make the same choice:

They tried to make me over
In their images.
Like mother, like daughter
Like sister, like brother.

I would never be alone, they promised,
If I followed in their footsteps
Empty formless chaos of muddy, shoeless outlines
Imprints of non-beings. (*Wrenching*, unpublished poem)

In the face of such horrific forces what *devices* did Julia possess to oppose them, to follow *her truth*? She did not perpetuate this line of intergenerational abuse. However, her reasons for success transcended her personal attributes:

To name them—physical strength, fierce will, resilience, the
     ability to fight
Does not explain what came from beyond on my behalf
What had genuine feminine attributes and a soft touch
A long reach and a ceaseless love.

I would not have made it without Her
She who arrived to carry me away
Effortlessly removing me from my shocked and shattered body
And revealing to me the Other Place...
(*Wrenching*, unpublished poem)

Direct contact with the transpersonal healing power of the Divine Mother, Julia's strength of soul coupled with a strong personality, the strength of our relationship—all uniting to do battle with these dark forces—convey a mythic dimension to her story. Unbroken, she is consciously stepping into the role of *wounded healer*. The reclamation of her gifts to perceive and work with the life-force in the body has granted her skillful means *to serve other*. Considering the magnitude of this work, Julia's choice is a testimony to the efficacy of her own healing.

8

The Uninvited Guest

I FIRST MET BOB AT A GATHERING OF FRIENDS. He appeared quiet, introspective and somewhat shy. However, we quickly cut through the small talk and anxiety of first meetings to a deep discussion of awareness and self-observation. As I listened, I thought, "He must practice Buddhist mindfulness." But no, he neither followed a spiritual path, nor was he engaged in psychotherapy. He was a musician. Later that evening I heard him play the trombone and recognized a seasoned jazzman.

Subsequent to this meeting I learned of Bob's recent retirement from teaching music, as well as his history of recording and performing with several jazz ensembles. He intended to devote himself to his music, teach in a literacy program and play more tennis. He intended to enjoy life.

Several years later Bob consulted me about a radical change in consciousness—a change that disrupted his life plan and left him grasping for sanity. This alteration of consciousness opened the door to an ongoing challenge of living in two worlds—one, his familiar, personal consciousness, the other, a vast field of awareness where his little self disappeared. The impetus for discovering this field, this uninvited guest, was neither a spiritual nor a psychological quest.

It was music.

Early in his musical education, Bob studied with a teacher who had discovered a method of understanding and classifying music emerging from the unconscious. His approach demanded great discipline and concentration wherein the student had to go slowly, and understand every step of the way in order to perceive the whole creative picture. Bob followed this practice for three or four years, but found it too demanding. Regretting, however, his earlier abandonment of a study designed to access greater understanding, he returned to this method after retiring.

He believed that this intense concentration created an opening to transpersonal realms. Jungian psychology posits that encoded in recurring dreams is a blueprint of our life. Bob had this recurring dream:

> Again and again I dream I am playing a B-flat to get the purest note possible. I know if I can play a pure note, it will carry me through.

He explained that each note has a *center* which emits a particular vibration. Striking the center of the note conveys a sense of balance; playing off center produces the opposite. This attempt to discover the pure note symbolizes Bob's passage from the fragile center of personal consciousness to the *stillpoint* of transcendent consciousness.

Six years into his journey, we had the following conversation:

Arya: Six years ago you underwent a very dramatic experience—the influx of a very different consciousness. How did that happen?

Bob: I began studying the piano, using the demanding method I had learned in my twenties—I don't mean just rapping away with my hands. I had been putting off playing this way for a long time. As I was playing I began thinking I was not really *in* it, no longer in contact with the small part of me. Rather, I was watching myself play it! I asked myself, "Why am I so detached? I'm playing Beethoven and I might as well be playing Chop Sticks." I got very depressed. My strongest feeling was that of being off-balance. Then I began to experience physical symptoms. An intense energy and heat filled my head creating a huge pressure, demanding my attention and a retreat from normal activities. I discovered I could release this pressure by sitting and focusing on the area of pressure and disorientation. There was an urge for my eyes to roll up. When I allowed this movement and concentrated on the upper part of my head, I could get some relief.

A. Is this a psychological release as well as physical?

B. It's physical. So at first, I thought this would be resolved by a physical explanation.

A. Surgery or a pill would have been preferable to your ordeal?

B. I was hoping it would be a brain tumor so they could chop it out. Then I wouldn't have been so puzzled. I thought I was going insane!

A. What were your main fears of going insane?

B. That I wouldn't be able to keep it together. I might not know what road I was on. I did not wish for spirituality. I already thought I was a spiritual person. I was not aspiring to be a yogi. Call it what you want—personal or impersonal. This is a physical phenomenon of energy. I should go to a yoga camp and forget about everything, including trying to balance this shit out. Sometime I think I should simply be sitting on a bench, staring.

A. Someplace where you are protected and don't have many duties?

B. Yes, where I don't have to show up some place at a certain time. Where I don't have to worry about crossing the street against the light and getting smacked by a car. It's become such an effort to keep it together!

A. It sounds like trying to live in two worlds at the same time, each pulling in a different direction.

B. I can think I am keeping it together, and in an instant I'm not.

A. In our previous conversations you spoke of a *magnet* pulling you out.

B. I follow my vision and the path of the energy leading from my forehead. If I go to the wall, *I go through it*. It feels like electricity.

A. You are touching your forehead when you say that.

B. The top part of my forehead is usually heated. When I wake up in the morning, it is intense. I have this sound in my ears, like cicadas. Sometimes I can disregard it. If I meditate, I can release it. However, if I have demands made on me, it is very difficult. Kate is understanding. She has become very sensitive to my experience. But she has to deal with her own energy. If I am in this state and she is talking to me, it becomes hogwash—like a fly buzzing around.

A. Do you allow yourself to be pulled out into that other space?

B. I have no choice. It can even happen when I'm walking down the street or playing tennis. I seem to go where my eyes are going—to *my real psyche*. When I do that, I can become the chair or the table. There is very little of my self left.

A. You are referring to your ego or personality?

B. Yes.

A. When you follow your vision, you get to the *real part of your psyche*. How do you know it's the real part?

B. I feel it in my body. There is a flow of energy and my body is lighter. There's a removal of tension.

A. When you go into this space, do you have a different awareness?

B. Yes.

A. Can you describe it?

B. If I wanted to be pompous, I could say it's *resignation* ... of the little emotional stuff in life.

A. In your ordinary consciousness?

B. In my ordinary life! All the emotional crap! We're all still going through the same crap we went through when we were three, two, one year old—it's just a repetition. *We're locked in a prison of darkness. It's a fucking prison*!

A. When you step out into this other space—is it different?

B. It wouldn't be different if someone punched me in the nose. I'm not trying to diminish the human struggle and what we have accomplished. My body hasn't yet gone completely into the other consciousness. But I have actually stepped into it. I am only participating in this ego because I *have this little personal life*. It's pretty confusing! A detachment like no other detachment. I'm on this side, but I think I'm on the other side. (Laughter) I'm here, but I'm not here.

A. How are these two selves connected?

B. It's like two wires touching, allowing me to pass back and forth. These wires only truly separate when we die, then it becomes very peaceful. I know this sounds like crap—it's the electricity of the universe or the environment—whatever! I'm connected somehow, but I don't know that it's permanent.

A. We were talking last time about this magnet that pulls you out into a different consciousness. What do you experience there?

B. I experience a real divorce from the everyday stuff—from my self, my persona, all the familiar emotions, the ego crap that gets you through the day. This everyday consciousness is no match for the other consciousness. I guess people meditate to get out of themselves and into it. But *I am in it*—in an energy field, similar to the energy field reportedly surrounding advanced yogis and saints. I can be a long way from my head—in the trees, in the sky, many places. I don't take off from the ground with my body, but with my psyche. It's in an altered ... *sea of consciousness* is a term that Gopi Krishna uses that I like. All of a sudden I'm transported out of myself. I'm getting good at this. I can do it in many places, anytime.

A. Even when you are moving?

B. Yes. Walking down the street. I know that I have a body that is walking; but I have to remember that, because I am in a place of heat, energy. If you sat down and concentrated on all the places on earth where it is night and day—on the stars, the moon ... it's like that. You think your little self is the center of what you are doing, but it isn't. We are fortunate enough to have this glue that holds us together in our small worlds, but there is a hole in the bottle. If the hole gets bigger and you go through it into this larger space, you will have a difficult time staying glued to your little self.

A. You mentioned this *sea of consciousness*. Is this a wider consciousness? Are you aware of a lot more things?

B. Solid awareness. *Awareness* is the only word I've found that describes this. Someone will say, "Awareness of what?" I can't answer that. For me it's awareness of something I really don't understand. *But the feeling is an awareness of everything.* It is what moves this human blob. It's a *center point*. All of a sudden, there it is *in one wordless place*. My abiding question is: *If I'm there, am I also here?* Of course I'm still here, but what is the *I'm* I am talking about? Is it the part that's keeping me from lifting off the planet? What is keeping me here? This is not clear to me. The spiritual books refer to self as witness, observer. I think there is a self that's just a light connection— personal or impersonal—it keeps us moving even when we have no experience of a center. Insane people move even though their psyche is off track. They dress themselves; they walk down the street. There is some force that keeps them going, but the upstairs part is gone. *My upstairs part is gone too!*... but not really.

A. Do you mean your ego?

B. No.

A. What do you mean by *upstairs part*?

B. The upstairs part is the part that has no ego. It's energy or electricity, a magnet. It comes from outside. It connects to me, but it belongs to this vast space.

A. Outside?

B. Not really outside, but outside my skin. For example, I can project this energy onto the wall. I sit in my apartment where there are cracks on the ceiling. I concentrate on one spot and eventually the spot divides into two. They move apart and finally disappear.

A. Where is your consciousness when they disappear?

B. I leap into another dimension. My head is always in more than one place. Although we may not be aware of it, this is true for all of us. We are always seeing a lot more than we *think* we see. We only absorb a small part. This is an impersonal observation.

A. Who is making the observation?

B. Who the hell knows? I don't even know *what* the observation is! I saw a movie called *What the Bleep Do We Know?* The subject matter is seeing in more than one dimension. They draw on theories of modern physics. I don't know anything about physics. I only know my experience. I can be sitting on a bench and I see a passing parade of the city's entire existence. A man walks past and I see him parading thirty years later. It is both the same person and not the same person.

A. When you are in this larger space of consciousness, what happens to your normal thought process? Normally, thought forms are always passing through.

B. It depends on the intensity of the consciousness, and the presence of other people. When others are present, I am in two places at once. I'm way out, but they think I'm with them. I can't be! Well, sometimes I can be emotionally with them ... sometimes. But I don't have the normal response mechanisms to the flow of life.

A. You don't have the common emotional responses to life?

B. Not to the small personal things that make life important to everyone. This creates problems.

A. It depends on the person.

B. Yes. I can respond. I'm not totally dead. But sometimes I'm not able to respond.

A. How does the wider consciousness affect your emotions?

B. I don't have any emotions when I'm in that field.

A. The emotional being quiets down?

B. It disappears. It could come back in a minute if someone threatened me with a gun. But if there is a natural flow, my emotional life disappears.

A. Are you more detached in that state?

B. They talk about cosmic consciousness—I'm not detached from that, but I am from the ordinary life.

A. What is your experience of cosmic consciousness?

B. I am in a non-personal, out-of-my-body place. *I am out of my personal history.* I can come back in an instant, but mostly I return by degrees. I haven't been the same for years. I have never come back to who I once was. I probably never will.

A. Is that beneficial for you?

B. It's more honest.

A. In the beginning of your experience, your biggest fear was not coming back to your ordinary consciousness.

B. I tell you, I think I was in extra-ordinary consciousness *before* I went out there. Whatever forced it, I went where I really am. I never was a regular fellow. I'm not responsive, emotional, ego-centered. I can be but... I have all the compartments that human beings have from the lowest to the most self-aggrandizing, but it's all history now. Still, I've tried to live in the ordinary consciousness, but it has been wiped away.

A. Can you see your personality—all the compartments—more clearly from the new consciousness?

B. Of course. Here's what happens when I'm by myself: If I don't filter my thoughts in dialogue— imaginary dialogues, *I have no thoughts!* I have observations, I have awareness, but I don't have inner dialogue. My brain wants a dialogue—it wants to see *me, small me, Bobby,* in a dialogue taking care of business one way or the other. Often my thoughts are filtered—some are filtered through my dialogue with you; my attempt to make my relationship work with Kate is a dialogue. It's difficult to realize that the insights I sometimes have in these dialogues are probably not going to affect any relationship. If I could have the courage to present them directly and honestly, perhaps, some small understanding could result. Mostly, I think the inner dialogues are self-serving.... *These dialogues are bad habits!*

A. Generally, the dialogues you have are with your self?

B. Yes. They are preparation and survival dialogues. Basically, a thinking process to prepare myself to meet some challenging situation. I read about an autistic child who at the age of thirteen was able to tell someone about his thought processes. He described dialoguing with himself to prepare for what he imagined was going to occur. When I prepare for a task, I think it through, so when my body is there doing it, I won't be totally lost. I do that when I'm going to be with Kate; I *prepare myself* to go on duty—I program the meeting so it will work out.... When I don't dialogue with anyone I become a different person—someone who is not afraid. *This other consciousness does not allow dialogues—I'm way beyond the dialogue.*

A. You can't make plans?

B. Nothing is going on! Sometimes there are musical patterns unfolding in my head, but if I really concentrate I can eliminate them.

A. No thought forms in your consciousness?

B. Nothing but heavy energy.

A. How do you experience this heavy energy?

B. My brain and my forehead feel stimulated.

A. A flow of energy?

B. Flow is another way of putting it. It's a special kind of concentration where I gather forces from all over. It feels like a life's work or the kind of concentration a yogi possesses to raise a ball from the floor to the ceiling.

A. What is the focus of your concentration?

B. I concentrate on a certain spot. When all the scattered forces come to this spot, I integrate them into a whole. *We are all together in that point.* This can last for two, five, ten minutes. Once I'm there, I go into trance—I don't like that word. Remember the stories you told me about the Mother going into trance with her teacup poised in midair. Well, I do that. I'm actually gone and my body is frozen in one position. This is beyond a concentrated place—intense heat and energy is present. If you put your hand on my forehead, it's hot. I've looked at pictures of yogis and they have this particular look in their eyes: *It's like the energy of another consciousness has got them by the balls. I see these guys looking just like I feel.* They are transfixed. They are trapped. I'm not totally trapped because....

A. So you think they're trapped?.

B. Call it free—if you want! They are in another place either by choice or.... They are not fighting it! There! Maybe I would be "free," too, if I lived in another culture. If I had been raised in a different way, I would be that kind of person.

A. So maybe you are becoming *that* without living in another country?

B. But I've got everything—pleasures, comforts, a companion, machines. I'm trying to keep everything—keep the whole thing together. For me, the very best situations exist when I don't have to figure anything out and I know that Kate is at peace with what I'm doing. If I didn't have to pretend or fight or be anything other than who I am ... this would help me! I've thought about taking the extreme action of isolating myself. But do I have to isolate? Sometimes, I think it is the only thing I *can* do to keep from offending people. Am I short-changing Kate if I cannot respond to her needs? I can't fulfill the needs of others. I don't feel capable! I work hard at it, though: For public appearances, I feel obliged to be dishonest. If I am honest, I seem to offend people.

A. What is the relationship between the heat in your head and the other consciousness? When you go out, does the heat increase or decrease? Is the heat a signal that the other consciousness is coming?

B. If I don't focus on this other place, my head becomes overwhelmed with heat and pressure. If I don't go there during the day, then in sleep It awakens me, my head buzzing with the loud sound of cicadas.

A. Are these the signals for needing to go into the other consciousness?

B. Yes. I need to follow the process of going there, not paying attention to any other matter. If I ignore this need, I pay a high price. I want to describe the episodes of projection—I believe they're electrical—in my dream/waking state. I've experienced them four times. If I was a yogi who had studied for ten years, this experience would have been his first lesson. You know I've been through a lot....

(Bob becomes very emotional)

A. When you cry now, what are you experiencing?

B. The memory of the day when the projection first occurred. Some of these experiences are tough (crying).... I'm pretty confident that I am going to come through, but they are horrible ... very bad!

A. Are these experiences from the distant past?

B. I experience dark places on this journey. I've been there, gone through them and I know when it is going to happen ahead of time. But it's still a helpless feeling—not knowing if you're going to be strong enough to get through it. Sometimes I put off dealing with it until I can be alone.

A. What do you see in the dark places?

B. I see monsters. It's like having a nightmare. It's so real that when I waken I am amazed!

A. Is it personal or impersonal?

B. It's personal in the sense that it is a part of my psyche. It is the experience of the dark monsters in Joseph Campbell's mythology books. They are really out there and I am out there without a rope to pull myself back. Having been through this does not make it easier when I have to pass through again. I buried this part for my entire life. Now, I am not able to bury it! (Crying)

A. All the yogic traditions speak about the necessity of a purification in order to receive the higher consciousness. The recipient is aware of the darkness as well as the light.

B. It's working in its own time! I'm only a vehicle! I'm not a yogi—I haven't sought this! I don't have a big enough persona to have any control! (Crying)

A. This is way beyond the persona. Thank you for sharing so much!

B. You've asked, "If you had a choice, would you tread this path?" No! I wouldn't!

A. Many people following a spiritual path expect a "bed of roses."

B. I don't know if this is a spiritual path. I don't have a fixed language to describe it. But nobody would choose the dark part! Everybody thinks about the "white light"—that's what they think meditation is about. It might be for some people, but it hasn't worked out that way for me. I've read enough to know, however, that the dark part is a part of this passage ... it's real for me. (Crying)

Anyway ... back to the dreams. I'm not sure they are dreams. I know I was present whether I was awake or dreaming. The *first dream* was pleasant. I saw the following projection on the ceiling of our bedroom: It was shaped like a mandala and in it leaves were flowing, as if I was looking into a stream with vegetation. I thought I was asleep. It was an unusual dream because it was projected onto the ceiling. Was I awake? The *second dream* was also in the shape of a mandala projected onto the ceiling in shades of grey, but not so pleasant. It was more organic with little worm-like shapes wriggling around—a bit disgusting. The *third dream* was like the second and my confusion persisted about being asleep or awake. The *fourth dream* was the experience of an electrical phenomenon. This projection was a large area of moving patterns of varying shades of gray with moving filaments and strands of light, some in the shape of resistors which were intermittently bright, glowing white, occurring in random spots. I could see and feel the electrical flow emerging from my forehead to create the pattern on the ceiling.

A. As if something in you was creating this?

B. I was a projector. I felt I was awake doing this. Well, could I turn it off without going back to sleep? I did.

A. How?

B. I don't know—I willed it. I guess it faded. When it disappeared, I was awake.

A. Did you experience this energy in other parts of your body?

B. No. It was amazing. There I was, a rod for this current! The *final dream* started like the previous one—an electrical projection. I knew I was awake. As it unfolded I thought, "I don't want to do this anymore. I'm calling this back!"

A. Did it scare you?

B. I had enough of it. I withdrew the projection. However, since these experiences, I have given this place in my head much more attention. I have surrendered to this consciousness: It takes the ball and runs with it. I just follow the magnet!

A. When you say "your head," do you mean your whole forehead?

B. My forehead on up to the crown of my head. It feels like having a cap on my head, similar to people who are being electrocuted! The real hot spot is in the middle of my brow.

A. So when you follow the trajectory of the magnet, you go out from your forehead.

B. It's similar to the projection onto the ceiling, only it goes further. This energy flow goes into a larger field of consciousness. Generally, I'm in a ball of this energy, but if I'm totally involved in a grounding activity, like cutting wood or playing tennis, I'm identified with my personal consciousness. However, when I play music, I *can't* use my mind to concentrate. I can't ask myself, "What are these four bars made up of?"... and then recall it. I can't do that. Music triggers a *yoga kind of thing.*

A. What is this *yoga thing?*

B. I have immediate access into the higher consciousness through the sound. If you are in a cathedral and the bells are ringing, eventually you will surrender to the sound. Music itself—not the composition—is a wordless place. When you are in the flow, it's a wordless place.

A. Does the sound activate the energy?

B. Participating in the sound does it. Although, with the piano, playing is on automatic, and as I play, I can be in a million other places.

A. What you are playing is not intentional?

B. It's improvisational. It's James Joyce in sound. It's flow of consciousness without words.

A. Is there some conscious intention to improvise? Or is someone else playing the music?

B. There is a history of improvising in my head. But music has a center and, when you go there, the music directs itself. Certain vibrations seem to go together. You can create dissonance. If you are beyond the repetitive patterns you have learned— beyond consonance—then the music can take you to many different places. You can control it. But I don't try to do that anymore. I've given music the place of a *yoga stimulus.* This is the one place I am solitary and I don't have to get permission to go there. Whatever it does for me or I for it, it's okay.

A. Does it ground you?

B. Yes, it's my life center. Early in my life I had this recurring dream. I had to learn to play a really pure B-flat. If I could learn to play this one, pure note, it would carry me through.

A. Is it a center?

B. That's right! Striking the center of the note gives a different vibration than striking off center. You get the sense you are in balance.

A. When you go out into this larger field of consciousness, do you discover a center?

B. Bernadette Roberts, the author of *The Experience of No-Self*, described it as a *stillpoint*. I call it a *balance-point*—when everything vibrates in balance. It's an all-inclusive point.

A. No separation?

B. It's all-inclusive. I can be a tree or a stepladder, as much as I can be a person. There is no *me*—there is a life force. I can be a leaf floating in the wind. I have no ego strength. I'm helpless!

A. I know you have read a number of books on consciousness and spirituality since your own experience has unfolded. Have these books helped? Do they give you a sense that you're not....

B. That I'm not nuts?... But I'm out there! And these people are too—very far out! They describe similar experiences, each in his own way. Ken Wilber is a brilliant, genius mind who also describes his personal experiences. And Aurobindo has got twenty years alone in a room. If you don't come up with something after twenty years, what the hell are you doing in there? You'd get goddam bored. (Laughter) Obviously, he *chose* to be there and wanted to go as far as he could. Fortunately for us, he described it. He went as deep as anyone can go. I never forget that I am a beginner. My experiences are both strong and convincing now; but still, by habit, I short-circuit or stop them. I'm still trying to manage the balance/imbalance problem, and I understand that this doesn't allow the experience to evolve into a whole. I never wanted to be a person who was totally eaten up by something. That's the reason I abandoned doing music in the way that could have brought the greatest results. The real performers are *consumed* by the music. This leaves them helpless in other areas. I didn't want to be trapped. Horowitz practiced ten hours a day. He drove himself nuts. It's physically demanding and the highest kind of mental concentration. I feel the same about the experience I am going through now.

A. You could be consumed by it?

B. That's my fear. When it comes so strongly, I feel, "O God, I'm finished, I'm gone!"

A. Is it stronger now? You have worked at bridging the personal consciousness with the transpersonal. Does this change the experience?

B. The energy in my head is stronger. In the beginning it used to come and go. It was struggling to push through my resistance. That was bad!

A. It still scares you?

B. No. I'm not afraid. It's more like having to run six miles when you know you will be exhausted after four. You have to travel the remaining two miles. It's the only way home. This is hard to face! God! Do I have to do this again and again? But I know I have to. I know what I have to face and try to use good judgment by not putting myself into situations (mainly social) that are too much to handle. I know the process now. If I give it space, it levels off.

A. So it's easier than in the beginning?

B. It's more familiar.

A. You know the terrain better?

B. It doesn't seem like that when it begins. Knowing doesn't do any good. It's like being out in a storm. You wait for it to subside so the water will be peaceful.

A. What are the major signals that you are moving into the other consciousness?

B. I can't concentrate, and my head is full of energy. The magnet starts pulling and I'm gone. I am drawn away from others and my surroundings. I'm in a wide place, and too much is happening at once for me to have any control.

A. You have to give in?

B. I give in. I'm getting good at it. I can be with others and they don't notice that I'm out.

A. They don't notice?

B. Even Kate forgets this is happening.

A. Does she understand that it goes on all the time?

B. She forgets. When it's extreme, she notices. I don't have normal human responses. She has responses that are over the top. It's amazing we're still together! But there is a reason two opposites attract. Kate has been a catalyst for involving me in life. She has exposed me to people and events. Left to my own desires, I would always choose solitude. I see myself sitting on a toadstool with my finger up my nose!

A. How does your personality appear from the vantage point of the other consciousness?

B. I don't just see *my* personality—I see *everybody's*. I see what we are all doing here!

A. You see more collectively?

B. I see everything. I've spent a lot of time self-examining, looking into this mirror.

A. How do you self-examine?

B. I sit down in a chair and the rattling begins. I just watch the rattling and I see all the shit I have carried around from day one to the present.

A. When you go out into the wider consciousness, does the *rattling* follow?

B. When I'm in the other consciousness, my personality is non-existent. I'm on automatic pilot. I don't have an identity. I'm a nothing.

A. You have no personal power?

B. Well, I don't walk in front of a car. If this other consciousness does what I think it does, you evolve out of your personality. I'm not the same personality I was, although I carry that personality. That's me in a former life. I'm still carrying its history. It gets me through and I'm emotionally tied to it. I enjoy the small things in life with that identity. It's the basis for pleasure and pain, but much of the time now I can't find either because I am gone.

A. No personality?

B. It's just sitting there. You leave your motorcycle at the curb and take the bus. The bus is taking me on a trip and I'm along for the ride. There is no itinerary. It's not a personal trip.

A. This consciousness is impersonal?

B. It's impersonal in the sense that it's beyond persona. Everything is impersonal to me. (Laughter) Still, I love people. I love you. I love Kate. I was on a bus the other day with many Mexican laborers and I felt close to them. My conditioning, my life history, the life-long personality that got me through in no way prepared me for this explosion of consciousness. My personality is not big enough to include this other consciousness; but it does not connect with the mainstream flow either. I cannot get with it. I can't imagine listening to what other people listen to; do what they do; think what they think.

A. Especially after being in the other consciousness.

B. Yes, it intensifies this feeling.

A. Doing self-examination and going out beyond personality are different levels.

B. Yes, I don't know the identity of the observer; but whatever it is, *that* is what I use in self-examination. The other consciousness takes me away. Sometimes it feels like samadhi. I swoon, but I'm not afraid that I will faint. It's beyond all the other experiences—beyond focus, concentration. *It just is and I am gone.*

A. The yogis distinguish between the quiet mind and the silent mind. In the former there are thoughts, but you are not identified with them. In the latter there is no thought.

B. My experience is more like the silent mind.

A. When you go there, what is your experience?

B. It's a relief. All the other shit is gone.

A. People who have near-death experiences describe going into another consciousness that's so calm and peaceful they don't want to return. Do you ever want to stay in the other consciousness?

B. I don't have thoughts about coming back or staying. I never fully come back anyway. I'm here on borrowed time.

A. You are in both places at the same time?

B. Yes. At some point all the mind stuff, analysis ... disappears. These operations of the mind occur even in the dream state, but in this other consciousness they completely disappear or are suspended.

A. You are at peace there?

B. I would say so. It's submission....

A. Is there a sense of time?

B. None. Simply, when I come back, I know where I've been. I come back relatively, but never totally. I think I've known this space since I was a small child. I probably went there to escape. That consciousness is the purest, most uncluttered state of being. All the other parts of me are there somewhere, but for the moment I have been given a reprieve.

A. Are you aware of your physical symptoms in that space?

B. They disappear. All discomfort is gone.

A. Are you aware of anything in particular in that space. You mentioned a *sea of consciousness*.

B. Not in that space. Sea of consciousness is associated with the magnet that pulls me out of my personal consciousness. *This other space is effortless.* These two levels are distinct.

A. Both Eastern and Western mystics distinguish between cosmic consciousness—awareness of the unity between all name and form—and transcendent consciousness—no form.

B. When I read books about the transcendent state, I wonder, "Are they talking about my experiences?" If I never read a book, it wouldn't matter. You told me I wasn't nuts! (Laughter) I am cautious about comparing other's experiences with mine. I don't want to pretend. But it doesn't matter anymore. For me, what is important is knowing I am not nuts and being able to get up and put my pants on in the morning.

A. And have a bagel! (Laughter)

B. A bagel and coffee.

A. When you are out in the field of consciousness with no awareness, is there a lot of energy?

B. No. It's not about energy: It's a release. It's wonderful.... But, I still wish I had a mind. I wish I could concentrate.

A. Feels like you "lost" your mind?

B. I have been overly occupied trying to figure out this experience with my mind. I've always felt that I don't know anything. Everybody else knows! When I was working at music, I only felt justified if I was explaining *what* I was discovering. I couldn't just follow the discovery... I still have this habit. Now, much of my inner dialogue is explaining my experience to you, to Kate, to Arasi. This dialogue is filtering my experience through someone who intellectually understands more than I do about it—who has a critical understanding of what I am trying to understand. Instead of following my own course, and feeling validated by the experience itself, I go to an "authority." I didn't really want to read these books on transcendence because I didn't want to filter my experience through a superior experience. I have to protect myself from being overwhelmed by my lack of judgment, experience, knowledge. I'm such a sucker; I could fall into anything!

A. You've been trying to verify your experience with something outside yourself.

B. Or, somebody! Somebody who already knows it. I'm filling in both the questions and the answers. Why do I have to do this?

A. It's all internal anyway.

B. Yes! It's my thinking process.

A. Now, what is your biggest fear?

B. That I'm going to be too far out to keep my life together. I'm afraid I will become totally unresponsive and will not be able to function if demands are made on me.

A. Despite the difficulty of this journey do you feel gratitude for this experience? Has it been beneficial?

B. I know I *should* feel gratitude. Sometimes I wonder what might have happened without the physical difficulties (pressure, heat). Maybe I would have evolved more naturally as I got older. I had a good plan for the remainder of my life, but this experience has disrupted everything. I had a very open mind about people's differences and possibilities. I would go out into the field and talk to God, "If you're up there, I'm ready! Fuck you, God. Do something about it!" But nothing happened and there I stood.... This experience is forcing me to take advantage of my deeper side, that part of myself that was always floating out there. Each day I felt good—sometimes exhilarated or ecstatic, whether it was music, looking at the sky or running. I had wonderful feelings; but when this other consciousness broke through, it wiped me out. I have very mixed feelings about being grateful. I had no choice. I wasn't prepared. I wasn't looking for it. I couldn't understand it. My partner was frantic about me all the time. I was in hell! Still I know the experiences are a big deal. I don't doubt that.

A. Are they beneficial?

B. Yes, I appreciate the insight and the awareness.

A. I know that language can distort and inflate experience, but how do you see this other consciousness?

B. My experience is one of the goals of meditation. You can call it nirvana or super-awareness. I am amazed by the power of the energy coming from my head. I always thought about the electrical energy in the air around us. If there is electricity coming through the outlets and through the sky, if there are electrical impulses in the brain, what is so unusual about human beings being connected to this energy? Everybody but you would think I'm a whacko for saying a magnetic force draws me out into a wider consciousness. That experience is quite remarkable—a *real* experience. It's an experience not of my mind, my thinking or analysis, not my projection—*it's a real, physical, psychological experience. Kundalini is a good term to use.* It's the description used in the books that makes the most sense. The results of that kind of energy take me to places to which many people aspire. I appreciate that! Usually,

I sit for two or three hours in the morning. Sometimes, I can't do anything else. I am besieged and I can't go out into this world.

A. When you wake up, are you already 'out'?

B. Yes, from sleep. For me the difference between sleep and waking is the presence of the personal self in waking—a self that can observe the activity. Sometimes, I waken and feel like a regular person, but then I become aware of the buzzing sound. I think it is the kundalini.

A. Kundalini does have a physical component.

B. Yes, the sound is like cicadas.

A. Does it go on all day?

B. Pretty much. It subsides when I am distracted, but if I sit quietly, it's as strong as the external sounds. It is a familiar sound now, except in the morning.

A. When you sit and get yourself together, do you become more identified with your personal consciousness?

B. No, I try to balance them. I try not to interfere with the activity in the upper part of my head. If I do, there is a battle all day.

A. Are you accepting the wider consciousness?

B. Yes.

A. Do you accept it as part of your self—part of your reality?

B. Yes. I don't think others will want it. I doubt whether it is something I can sell.

A. For six years I have watched you go through a passage that often brought you to the edge of sanity. Many others might have lost it.

B. Yes, this is true.

A. You have found the strength to accommodate a monumental change of consciousness.

B. I have a lot of endurance. I go along as if that is what I'm supposed to do because I don't know any better. I am strong.

A. Do you have permanent access to the new consciousness?

B. I don't know about permanent, but I do have ready access. I'm there—I can't go back from there. I can temporarily distract myself, and I do. I enjoy not being on the mountain. I enjoy getting rid of my change, my pennies, cutting wood, getting the right amount of peanut butter off the knife.

A. Simple pleasures!

A. Are you in your personal consciousness and the other consciousness at the same time?

B. Yes, but there are degrees. The new consciousness is there all the time. However, I would be happy to let *it* go! My internal system has been altered; it will never be the same.

A. What if the new consciousness disappeared?

B. I am troubled mostly by the physical symptoms—pressure, heat—what I perceive as energy. If that ceased and I woke like most people and sat down to meditate, what would I experience? I believe that where I go is not a product of my imagination. I did not make it up. It is a permanent experience. However, I would be happy to let go! If this intensity would leave my head and it was a more peaceful path ... that would be okay. The energy is too distracting, sometimes distressing. Although I am better at dealing with it now, it wipes out my concentration and my personality.

A. Does the new consciousness ever enhance your activities?

B. Yes, when I play music, I draw on the best stuff that is in there. There is no interference from the mind. Using the mind does not work. I have to get out of the way and let it roll.... When I am playing tennis, as soon as the competitive ego steps forward, I'm finished. Then I say, "Let's go back to how you were playing a minute ago—just chase the ball and don't care about the score."

A. So if you can keep your ego out of it...

B. I don't keep anything out of anything anymore. I just recognize it for what it is. I just play the game for the rhythm and the feel and the dance!

A. How does the new consciousness effect your involvement in music?

B. I was always trying to analyze what I heard so I could use it. Now, I can't analyze it, so I hear more dimensions. The really great performers go beyond the thinking part. They do their work of thinking, analyzing, but then they let it go and allow the power of the music to use them. Others have the training, the skill, but they cannot access the magic.

A. But you have to prepare the instrument in order to receive something?

B. Yes, it's like a track star. He trains and trains, but on the day of the race he lets go. I trained my psyche through music.

A. This amazing journey began with music.

B. *Music blew it open. The piano study blew it open. I got stretched too far by this other consciousness. It popped a button!*

A. You said, "If this consciousness does what I think it does, you evolve *out* of your personality." After living with this consciousness for six years, what, in your personality, needs the most work to facilitate this evolution?

B. My personality is like everybody else's. I want to be Mr. Wonderful, to be satisfied, to be fulfilled, to be able to perform perfectly. Also, there are good feelings—like finishing a carpentry job. And bad feelings—like when I was young, I had this fantasy of machine-gunning people I didn't like! (Laughter) The fear in us wants all these attachments as support.... One of the major obstacles, however, in facilitating this evolution is my belief that no one has the capacity to know any answer. People say the divine this, the divine that, the Him God, the Her God. This is all human concoction. Maybe it derived from an experience of higher consciousness, but the interpretation is human! I don't get the *God feeling*. I get powerful feelings, but I don't know the real story. I've given up on *knowing,* or trying to figure out who did the Big Bang.

A. Are you saying you don't have absolute knowledge?

B. I feel I can get to the center of my psyche which I feel is the center of everything, but this may also be a mental concoction.

You see, I'm a skeptic. I envy people who have religion. I never had it. And this leads me to the other major obstacle interfering with this consciousness—*my bad attitude.*

A. What do you mean?

B. *I don't have God-Consciousness.* I read a book about the visions of Ramakrishna. He speaks of these visions in religious terms. I believe in his experience, but cannot bring myself to call it "God." I believe in the force of nature and electricity. I believe in the story you told me about St. Theresa being thrown out of bed by the kundalini and balancing on the top of her head. I believe in universal power, but I don't have an interpretation of these experiences. That leaves me loose and vague. The most I can say is: *I am touched by an awareness of a much deeper part of myself than I can understand.* But I don't have an interpretation.

A. In the beginning you were afraid of losing parts of your personality. Good feelings, things you enjoyed. Is that fear still present?

B. I found a way to still access little pleasures. I tickle myself, laugh at little things. This happens when I am alone. Mainly, I don't want to be a fraud. The warnings are in all the books: Don't become self-satisfied with your special qualities. They are nothing! Besides, I have a mirror and I see all the shit that comes up. I say, "You fool!"

A. This happens when you practice self-examination?

B. I don't have to be sitting. It's constant! But I can't immediately cleanse myself. I can't take a knife and cut out the bad parts. I have to endure them. I've spent so much time sitting by myself—my self-awareness is very strong. But, I'm a beginner.

*   *   *   *

After our conversation, I kept returning to Bob's story of going out in a field to call and challenge God. "If you are up there, I'm ready!" and "Fuck you, God! Do something about it!"

Mystical literature is filled with accounts of the aspirant's desperate or angry cry for revelation—*the call*. And then the *response* coming in a time, a space, a form, unpredictable and unimaginable.

Bob would be loathe to call this invasion of a new consciousness God. Yet the total disruption of his life, and near-annihilation of his personal consciousness are classic initiatory marks of the passage through the portals of *mystical experience*. Without knowledge and awareness of this initiation, these marks might be mistaken for insanity.

Bob grappled with terror of insanity for the first two years of his journey. Trapped in a mind unable to concentrate and perform its usual analytic operations, he suspected the worst. He was walking on a razor's edge: On the one hand, testing for organic dysfunction and making decisions about medication; on the other, slowly embracing the process of this strange, new consciousness.

Bob was in the midst of a *spiritual emergency*. Had he sought the help of someone unfamiliar with the signs of an evolving consciousness, this process might have been aborted by medication/hospitalization. Although frequently overwhelmed by the foreign terrain of his passage, he clung to a sense of meaning and direction. Despite external pressure to seek temporary respite, Bob *chose* to allow a consciousness that threatened to obliterate his familiar identity.

The evolution from an ego-centered identity (personal consciousness) to a universal identity (cosmic consciousness) to an identity beyond name and form (transcendent consciousness) is the journey of the mystic and the yogi. Not only has Bob experienced the dissolution of boundaries between these three poises of consciousness, but a frightening confusion regarding his own identity. Who is this shifting "I"—chair, tree, star—this human form called "Bob"? Early on, he found solace in the following:

We have identified ourselves with our body, mind and personality, imagining these objects to constellate our real "self," and we then spend our entire lives trying to defend, protect, and prolong what is just an illusion. We are the victims of an epidemic case of mistaken identity, with our Supreme identity quietly but surely awaiting discovery. And the mystic wants nothing more than to have us awaken to who, or what, we really and eternally are *beneath* or *under* or *prior to* our pseudo-self. Thus he asks us to cease identifying with this false self.... My mind, my thoughts, my desires—these are no more my real Self than the trees, the stars, the clouds, and the mountains.... What I am goes much, much beyond this isolated, skin-bounded organism. (Ken Wilber, 1985, p. 57)

Bob has been propelled beyond his ordinary consciousness by an energy which creates heat and pressure in his head. In the early stages of his passage, these physical symptoms triggered intense headaches and depression. It was the force that opened his inner vision (projection of mandalas) and transported him into the *sea of consciousness,* and beyond. Many of its manifestations bear strong resemblance to *kundalini energy,* long experienced by mystics of East and West. The recipients of this evolutionary energy bear testimony to its power to break any resistance (in personal consciousness) that prevents movement towards the universal and transcendent. Insistence on clinging to these formations can create intense physical and psychological suffering. This force of *kundalini* demands nothing less than total surrender.

Bob has recounted many instances of facing the dark parts of his personality. Despite his suffering, however, he recognized them as obstructions. Equally difficult has been his reluctance to let go of his retirement plans—innocent plans to enjoy life. His early attempts to ignore the manifestation of this new consciousness led to great pain and suffering.

He has experienced many signs germane to an arousal of *kundalini*—the energy of consciousness. The initial symptoms were *intense energy, heat and pressure* in his head (covering his forehead to the crown). These physical phenomena were accompanied by great *detachment,* as well as *fear, anxiety and depression.* Bob discovered *single seeing* to relieve the extreme pressure in his head. This aspect of *kundalini* is achieved by gradually rolling the eyes upward and centering on the crown of the head. Eventually, this special concentration allowed him to go from personal to universal to transcendent consciousness. He also entered *deep trance states* wherein his body was locked into particular postures. For several years Bob has experienced the abiding *sound of cicadas*—a classical phenomenon of *kundalini.* Finally, his *electrical projections of mandalas* correspond to the inner lights and visions of *kundalini.* (Sannella, 1992)

Often, the awakening of *kundalini* is transitory, ultimately leaving one's consciousness unchanged. Often, it can be aborted by an external force such as medication. For the last six years, Bob has never been free of this mysterious energy. It has exerted a constant pressure to enter a wider consciousness. Not only does he have ready access to the latter, but it is present, simultaneously, with his personal consciousness. Bob's ongoing battle to find a balance between a limited personal consciousness and a limitless, impersonal one is a work in progress.

He is drawn from his personal consciousness by a magnetic force (*kundalini*) and transported to his "real psyche." His description of this state corresponds to what mystics call *cosmic consciousness.* Here the tension in his body disappears as well as the pulls of his personality. In this *sea of consciousness*—a place of *solid awareness*—Bob can become the chair, the table, a star: "There is very little of my self left." Here the awareness is

...of something you really don't understand. *But the feeling is an awareness of everything....* It's a *center point* for all the complicated things in the mess. All of a sudden, there it is in *one wordless place.*

This cosmic perspective allows Bob to witness all the compartments of his personality. Here he stops filtering his thought through *imaginary dialogues*. "This other consciousness does not allow dialogues. I'm way beyond dialogue."

Beyond the transcience of ego-centricity, Bob discovered another center: "I call it a *balance-point*. There everything vibrates in balance. It's an *all-inclusive point*." From this center he can assume many forms.

> It's an all-inclusive form. I can be a tree or a stepladder as much as I can be a person. There is no *me*—there is a life-force that can create anything.

This fluidity of form reflects the mystic's cosmic consciousness wherein ... "One begins to feel others too as part of oneself or varied repetitions of oneself, the same self modified by Nature in other bodies." (Sri Aurobindo, 1995, pp. 316-17)

Bob also entered another field of consciousness where name, form and awareness were absent. "It just is and I am gone." No personality, no thought, no emotions, no identity. All discomfort disappears and he is at peace. This state resembles *yogic trance (samadhi)*—... a complete trance in which there is no thought or movement of consciousness or awareness of either inward or outward things—all is drawn up into a supracosmic Beyond." (Sri Aurobindo, 1995, p. 741)

These parallels between mystic/yogic and Bob's experience have not moved him towards interpretation. While they have alleviated his fear of insanity, he is adamant about *not* using terms such as "spiritual" or "God" to describe his experience.

In his youth, he and his family belonged to an evangelical, Christian church known for its emotional healing rituals. At eight or nine years he was called up to the front of the church to be healed. Kneeling and closing his eyes, he waited and waited for God to come. Eventually, someone tapped him on the shoulder and said, "Everyone has gone." While this event did not endear Bob to organized religion, it revealed his perseverance and willingness to explore new experiences. At a very early age he may have unwittingly opened himself to mystical experience.

Bob did not invite his new consciousness to establish residency in his being. However, he now recognizes it as a familiar guest.

> When I come back, I know where I've been. I come back relatively, but never totally. I think I've known this space since I was a small child. I probably went there to escape. That consciousness is the purest, most uncluttered state of being.... I tell you, I think I was there before I went there. Whatever forced it—I went where I really am.

Bob continues to journey in uncharted territory. What lies ahead is veiled in mystery. One thing is clear: His consciousness has been radically and permanently altered. The *uninvited guest* has become a *resident*.

Epilogue

SUFFERING, THE PRODUCT OF HUMAN EXPERIENCE, can come in the form of relational issues, illness and death, trauma or spiritual emergency as it did for those in this book. Their healing journeys intersected and ultimately benefited from contact with the transpersonal or spiritual dimensions of the psyche. Though an earlier prototype of the psyche would have dismissed their experiences as pathological, the evolutionary, alchemical force of the soul is present in all human endeavor, including the field of psychology.

The stories of transformation presented here illustrate the acceleration of psychotherapy through the integral process of bridging the personal and transpersonal dimensions of consciousness. As we have seen, Carrie traced the origin of her terminal illness beyond scientific materialism as the emergence of her soul revealed a new life in the presence of death. Joan was freed from a barren relationship through past life experiences. Julia discovered transpersonal, healing forces in her assent from an underworld of torture and abuse. And Bob was compelled to cope with a cosmic, transcendent consciousness which was not part of his life plan.

In working with these experiences and others, I have felt the alchemy of the soul—the evolutionary force working to manifest a new center of consciousness in humanity. Unlike ego-centered psychology, soul-centered psychology offers an awareness of the inner as well as the outer world. It incorporates spiritual experience as an essential dimension of the human psyche. Sri Aurobindo takes this notion further by stressing the integral relationship between body, life-force, mind, soul and spirit.

As an integral healer, I approach healing with the understanding that each level of consciousness ultimately contains all others. This understanding incorporates:

1. a model of the human psyche possessing individual, universal and transcendent dimensions of consciousness as well as

2. a practice which recognizes the full spectrum of consciousness and its interdependent components. These components (body, emotion, mind, soul and spirit) which co-exist as energetic structures, differentiated only by vibrational frequencies, ultimately constitute an integrated whole.

In this context, all that presents itself in an integral, therapeutic session can serve in the process of evolving consciousness.

Conquest of the difficult terrain between an egocentric and soul-centered awareness requires skill in both psychotherapy and spiritual practice. This effort demands the integration of these domains to create a discipline which honors all parts of our being—a creation marking an outstanding achievement of conscious evolution. Although psychotherapy and spirituality have ignored each other in the past, presently we are witnessing the emergence of transformational psychotherapies which employ the full spectrum of consciousness—from body to spirit. The pioneering work of Grof, Mindell and Raheem in the integration of body and spirit with mind and life force has furthered a creative collaboration between once alienated practices. Efforts such as theirs, coupled with Sri Aurobindo's vision of a soul-centered individual opens a way for a radically new, evolutionary psychology. This opening possesses the power of joining body and spirit, ultimately giving birth to a greater psychology and a wider consciousness.

References

Almaas, A. (2000). *Facets of Unity: The Enneagram of Holy Ideas.*
Boston: Shambhala.

Dalal, A. (1991). *Psychology, Mental Health and Yoga.* Ohai, CA:
Institute of Integral Psychology.

Einstein, A. quoted in Capra, F. (1991). *The Tao of Physics.*
Boston: Shambhala.

Ford, C. (1989). *Where Healing Waters Meet.* Barrytown, N.Y.:
Station Hill Press.

Grof, S. (1985). *Beyond the Brain.* Albany: State University of
New York.

Hillman, J. (1997). *The Soul's Code.* New York: Warner Books.

Irving, D. (1995). *Serpent of Fire.* York Beach, ME: Samuel
Weiser.

Jung, C. (1989). *Memories, Dreams and Reflections.* New York:
Vintage.

Kornfield, J. (1989). "Obstacles and Vicissitudes in Spiritual
Practice." in Grof, S.&C. (Eds.). (1989). *Spiritual Emergency.* Los Angeles, CA.: Tarcher.

Kornfield, J. (1993). *A Path With Heart.* New York: Bantam.

Laing, R. (1965). "Transcendental Experience in Relation to
Religion and Psychosis." in Grof, S.&C. (Eds.). (1989).
Spiritual Emergency. Los Angeles, CA.: Tarcher.

Mindell, A. (1982). *Dreambody.* Boston: Sigo.

Moore, T. (1992). *Care of the Soul.* New York: Harper Collins.

Mother. (1951-1973). *Mother's Agenda.* (Vols. 1-13). New York: Institute for Evolutionary Research.

Mother.(1972-1987). *Collected Works of the Mother (CWM).* Pondicherry: Sri Aurobindo Ashram

Mother. quoted in Satprem. (1982). *Mind of the Cells.* New York: Institute for Evolutionary Research.

Ring, K. (1984). *Heading Toward Omega: In Search of the Meaning of the Near-Death Experience.* New York: William Morrow.

Sannella, L. (1992). *The Kundalini Experience.* Lower Lake, CA.: Integral Publishing.

Serrano, M. (1968). *Jung and Hesse: A Record of Two Friendships.* New York: Schocken.

Sri Aurobindo. (1987). *The Life Divine.* Pondicherry: Sri Aurobindo Ashram.

Sri Aurobindo. (1992). *The Synthesis of Yoga.* Pondicherry: Sri Aurobindo Ashram.

Sri Aurobindo. (1995). *Letters on Yoga. (Vols. 1-3).* Pondicherry: Sri Aurobindo Ashram.

Sri Aurobindo. (1996). *Savitri.* Pondicherry: Sri Aurobindo Ashram.

Sri Aurobindo. (2000). *On Himself.* Pondicherry: Sri Aurobindo Ashram.

Thich Nhat Hanh. (2000). *Anger.* New York: Berkeley Publishing Group.

Wilber, K. (1985). *No Boundary.* Boston: Shambhala.

Wilber, K. (2000). *One Taste.* Boston: Shambhala.

Woodman, M. (1993). *Conscious Femininity.* Toronto: Inner City Books.

Index

active imagination, 33, 69
Almaas, A. H., 44
Ammachi, 42
ananda, 36
archetypes, 20, 47-48, 56, 72
Assagioli, Roberto, 125
(Sri) Aurobindo, 4-7, 19-24, 42, 45,
    46, 49-66, 68, 72, 73, 75, 128,
    161, 178
    "The most dangerous man in
    India," 4
    and Jung, 48-50
awareness, 152

behaviorism, 1
body
    dreaming, 27-41
    container for personal history, 36
    ground for spiritual manifestation,
    36
    and psycho-spiritual process,
    25-41
    and soul, 13-16, 23-24
    transformation of, 5-6
    and transpersonal psychology,
    7-10
Buddhism, 7, 33, 48, 147
    and shamanism, 78-81

Campbell, Joseph, 157
cancer, 95-119
    living with, 103-104

chakras, 56
character, changing one's, 67-68
chi, experiencing, 105-107
Christianity, 8, 48
consciousness, 2, 3, 4, 51, 52
    altered states of, 74-78
    as sat, chit-sakti, ananda, 51
    cosmic, 5, 175
    divine, 6
    evolution of, 3-4
    five dimensions of, 50-51
    full spectrum of, 93
    higher states of, 2
    involution and evolution of, 50-53
    lower and upper hemisphere of,
    51-52
    paradigm for an integrated, 53-63
    personal, cosmic, transcendent,
    172
    psychical, 53
    spectrum of, 2-3
    spontaneous opening of spiritual,
    147-176
    supramental, 5
    without ego, 152-153
cosmic consciousness, 2, 5, 175
creation
    Western and Eastern conception,
    51

dance, healing power of, 137-138,
    140

181

About the Author

ARYA MALONEY, M.A. Clinical Psychology, has more than thirty years experience as a psychotherapist. His psychotherapeutic training includes family therapy, gestalt, process-oriented psychology, holotropic breathwork, and process acupressure. He has facilitated workshops on integrating personal and transpersonal psychology as well as body-centered psychotherapy in the United States, Europe and India.

Arya's approach to healing is integrative, following the person's unique process as it manifests in the physical, vital (emotions-sensations), mental and spiritual parts of the being. In this process-oriented therapy, body work and dream work mirror one another. While addressing a wide spectrum of problems, he specializes in trauma, issues arising from death and dying, and spiritual emergency.

Alchemy of the Soul: Integral Healing—The Work of Psychology and Spirituality is serialized in the Indian journal, *NAMAH*. A practitioner of the Integral Yoga of Sri Aurobindo and the Mother, he has published many articles on this spiritual discipline and is a co-founder of the Mindbody Centre in Kingston, New York.